SEARCH FOR MOTHER MISSING

A PEEK INSIDE INTERNATIONAL ADOPTION

JANINE VANCE

interior and exterior cover design concept:
copyright ©2005 contact@janinevance.com
Linoprint used for the cover: DariusXstudio.com

All rights reserved. This book or any part thereof may not be reproduced in any form whatsoever without prior permission of the author, except in the case of brief passages embodied in reviews or articles. Any distribution of unpublished versions of this book must be destroyed or at risk of facing criminal copyright charges.

Dedication

*to all human beings.
May we realize our authentic power and
make this world a better place for all.*

Gratitude

*I thank my family and friends
who gave loving support while I wrote.
The Mother of the Universe
has truly blessed me with their care.
Frederick Su & Elfi Hornby gave insightful advice and edits.*

AN "UNKNOWN" DUCKLING 10
GOOD NEWS 18
CHANGE IS A CONSTANT 24
CROSSING BOUNDARIES 30
SHOOTING BLANKS 2003 35
FIRST SUPPER 43
INFORMATION AGE 49
LIFESTYLES OF THE RICH AND FAMOUS 59
UNFORGOTTEN SONS 67
ONE NATION UNDER GOD 75
MYSTERY MAN 81
UNFORGOTTEN DAUGHTERS 87
A TASTE OF TEMPLE 93
OUR PLATES ARE FULL 99
MAN'S BEGOTTEN SON 105
AS NATURE MADE US 115
SEOUL SIBLINGS 123
I AM WAITING, LONGLONG TIME 130
TWO BIRDS IN THE BUSH 135
THE MISSING LINK 140
FREEDOM DAY 148
THE EMPEROR HAS NO CLOTHES! 155
CHILD SAVIORS? OR SAVIOR COMPLEX? 164
2023 NOTE FROM JANINE 172
ABOUT THE VANCE TWINS TODAY 181

Rooted

There is a thing inherent and natural,
Which existed before heaven and earth.
Motionless and fathomless,
It stands alone and never changes;
It pervades everywhere
and never becomes exhausted.
It may be regarded as Mother of the Universe.
I do not know its name
If I am forced to give it a name,
I call it Tao, and I name it as supreme.

--Lao-Tzu

Foreword

I am a seventy-seven-year-old adoptive father, and I write this for other adoptive parents. In 1972, my wife and I got twin baby girls born in Seoul, South Korea. When I got the twins, I had planned to take care of them, but in one of life's ironic twists, they ended up caring for me, and it turned out to be to my advantage.

I graduated from college in 1952 with a degree in physics. After I had married, I went right to work at The Boeing Airplane Company. I worked steadily for them until I was forced to retire as a result of a hang glider accident in 1984. My wife, the girls' adoptive mother, died of cancer in 1997.

Today, I live with one of my daughters, and I've always thought of them as my girls. It never occurred to me that my daughters might think about their birth parents or the Korean culture they left. When they told me they were going to look for their birth parents, at first, I feared I might lose them. Assuming the worst case, I thought that if they found their birth parents, they might leave me for South Korea.

However, nothing can change the past, and nothing can detract from the happiness I felt while raising them. Today, my goal is always to be happy. I decided to encourage them in anything they tried. I even urged Janine to write this book. Anything that makes my girls happy makes me happy. If they do find their Korean family, I will see it as a win-win situation. I'll just have gained a new family.

After the girls got back from South Korea, our relationship has been unchanged. The girls are still my daughters, and they still think of me as their dad. We still interact like a typical family. In my perception, their trip to Korea produced no adverse effects in our relationship, just additions, such as the recognition that we are more alike than different.

All I know for sure is that they are my kids. I am proud of Janine for all her hard work. I've read the book, and I think it's very well written, greatly informative, and enlightening.

We never throw away the past; we just add to it. As old as I am, I still learn, and I've recently become aware of things that have changed my whole outlook on life. Read this book and see if your perspective will change.

Rev. Dr. Allen L. Vance

An "Unknown" Duckling

A journey of a thousand miles begins with a single step.
—Lao-tzu

On the drive home from the grocery store, I spot the sign again: *Korea Post.* A surge of urgency runs through my blood. I've seen the local newspaper before but was too timid to actually go in. Only two weeks from now, my twin sister and I will be in Seoul, South Korea! As a stay-at-home mother of two and a caregiver to my disabled father, the upcoming trip is a rare opportunity to shift my attention to me.

The sign reminds me of my sister's comment. "Janine," she had said, confirming my trepidation, "Our trip to Korea might be the only chance we'll have at finding our birth parents. We might never go to Korea again."

Because I am of Korean ethnicity, most fellow Americans might think that I'm not a *real* American citizen. But I am. I haven't even explored my Korean roots, and I'm already thirty-two years old! I come from a white all-American family, so I've never identified myself as a *real* Korean. According to what I had heard while growing up, Asians were grouped into one odd flock. *They* were not wanted or needed and could migrate back to where *they* came from if *they* couldn't handle the weather here. According to "real" Americans, *modern-day immigrants* stole jobs from the beautiful "swans" born here. I assumed "real" Koreans ate gross food and got good grades. Why associate with foreigners?

When I was a child and only exposed to one flock, it was the refined and glorious "swans," and all other birds were perceived as mere ugly ducklings. I was supposed to follow my parents' footsteps and walk a specific "right-winged" path—because that's the kind of bird my parents wanted me to be, and that's how they flew.

My sister's comment runs through my mind again. *Our trip to Korea might be the only chance we'll have at finding our birth parents. We might never go to Korea again.*

Her comment motivates me to turn the van around. I've avoided the possibility long enough. Since it's now only two more weeks until we leave, I have to go inside! My heart pounds. I wonder if the newspaper staff will translate the letter I had written to our Korean mother in anticipation of the Adoptee Gathering. I want to get it into one of the major newspapers in Seoul, perhaps before our trip, so our Korean family might read it and meet us at the hotel. There could be a slim chance our biological parents have been looking for us; I'd want them to know we'll be in the area. I've been stashing my adoption papers and the letter to my birth mother in the van for weeks, just in case I found the time or the courage to actually walk into the office and ask for help. I know if my twin had the opportunity, she'd be right beside me. But she's at work—always at work in multiple nursing homes teaching patients how to regain their independence after an injury or surgery. She loves her job, and work keeps her busy.

I swerve into the parking lot that serves several professional offices, which face Puget Sound. A cool salty mist blows off the water and refreshes me as if a damp cloth placed on my forehead. I enter a large periwinkle building, where the *Korea Post* is accessible by an internal door located in a corridor and peer into a side window. The office environment is not rushed like newsrooms shown in American movies. In fact, it's the opposite. The two women hunched in front of computers look approachable.

Having rarely been around my own ethnic "flock of birds," I wonder how the women will receive me. I remember being around Korean women only once when I was a kid. My beautiful Caucasian mother had taken my twin and me to a Korean American church potluck. Following Mom, we felt uneasy at the table; it was the last time we socialized there. Those birds were too odd for our taste.

My beautiful adoptive parents tried to uphold all-American ideals. They believed in presenting themselves in the best of light. My dad collected American cars. My mom collected delicate white porcelain dolls. She wore beauty products from Avon and decorated the house from JCPenney and Sears sales. She dressed my sister and me in fluffy pastel Easter and red velvet Christmas dresses and Mary Jane shoes. We ate jarred spaghetti sauce over noodles or sweet and sour chicken over boxed Uncle Ben's rice. We ordered pizza on Friday nights.

My all-American parents believed it was their duty as "swans" to take us to church each week for activities such as Sunday school, youth group, and mid-week services—in a Cadillac Limousine, no less. My sister and I lit the candles on the front altar. My mom played the organ, my dad directed the choir. There was nothing Asian about us; we were the all-American swan family. I believed I was a typical American girl. My environment was all white. It was *I* who was wrong. It was *I* who did not match the flock of glorious swans.

I peek through the *Korean Post* window again and see the two Korean women sitting peacefully at their desks. Will they be offended that I don't speak the Korean language—the language I've been told by well-meaning adults that I'm supposed to know?

After a few moments of silence, I grab the chrome doorknob and muster together enough courage to tiptoe into the office.

Both Korean women raise their brows, startled at my sudden intrusion. The older one in the yellow dress stands. "May I help you?"

"Yes. I am looking for my birth parents." I intentionally speak out like a confident American. "I was adopted when I was a baby. There's going to be a huge adoptee Gathering—" I notice a man peek around the corner from a remote office. *Am I too loud?* I lower my voice. "Um . . . . There's going to be a conference in Seoul two weeks from now. I was hoping you could—"

The woman in the yellow dress stands from her desk and points at the front door, and then walks me toward it. I immediately assume she wants me out of the office, and my heart skips a beat. *Is she kicking me out already? Maybe I shouldn't be looking for my birth family. Maybe it's none of my business. Is it even normal for adoptees to look? Maybe I'm out of line.*

"Please have a seat," she whispers, pulling out a gray padded chair near a small round table.

Oh, relief. She's only taking me by the door to the table and chairs. Still, I feel guilty for wasting her time. Waiting for the woman to return, I twirl long feathered hair into knots with nervous fingers, wondering if I'm doing the right thing, wishing Jenette was with me instead of at work. I stare at the walls, naked with pale plaster as drab as a hospital gown. They seem to beg to be colored with more than a journalistic hand. After a minute, the woman returns with a pen and yellow legal pad. I explain that we will be in Korea for two weeks. At the same time, I spread the small number of documents I have on the table.

"Excuse me. May I read your letter?" The somber woman in yellow asks.

Sliding the letter toward her, I pray that she will somehow get this translated and sent to Korea.

To our Korean mother:
My twin and I will be at the Adoptee Gathering in Seoul, South Korea, this coming August, which will be our first trip to our motherland. We are very much looking forward to discovering our roots—something that has remained a mystery to us for all our lives. We would like to meet our birth parents. There is no anger or resentment, and you should not feel ashamed. We had a good life in America and consider ourselves to be very lucky. Even though you have not played a part in our lives, you have been with us on a subconscious level. Our adoptive mother passed away from cancer seven years ago, and our adoptive father sustained a head injury when we were twelve and is now disabled. It is now time to meet so that we may heal the past. Please e-mail us with any information you have. We look forward to getting to know you.
    Sending peace, love, and joy to Seoul,
    Janine and Jenette;-)*

While the Korean newspaper employee skims my typed letter, I see her swallow hard, and then I hear her breathe slowly. It's obvious that the message made an emotional impact. She jots notes and asks for our Korean names, being careful to get the spelling right. She motions me to follow her to the computer while she looks up websites that could possibly help us. At last, she finds Holt International's Korean website (the agency we were adopted through). A page with photos of adoptees looking for birth parents pops up. I had no idea other adoptees had the audacity to look. Thank goodness Jenette and I are not a rare case. As she scribbles Korean writing on the legal pad, she assigns the younger woman to scan Jenette's "Intake Form," the letter to birth parents, and her adoption papers into the computer. She e-mails these documents, along with my authorization, to Holt's Seoul office along with a note that Jenette and I will visit the Post Adoption Services Office in August. She also sends my permission to release whatever birth files are necessary upon our arrival. We're interested in visiting the street we were told to have been found on, according to Jenette's intake form, and visit the orphanage we were placed in.

The woman paws through a stack of files, finally pulling out copies of maps and directions to the buildings located in Seoul. We will only need to hand the map to the taxi driver. From her desk, she stops and studies me for an instant. "Don't give up hope. Reunions can happen," she reports. "A while ago, I helped an adoptee reunite with her father."

I am amazed that she is doing this for us. "Thank you," I say.

The woman in yellow silently follows me out the door, into the corridor, and then eventually to the parking lot. Once I reach my van, she surprises me with an outburst, "I'll be praying for you!"

I think to myself. "I did it!" It's the first time we've ever made a move to examine our past! It's the first time we've attempted to look for answers about ourselves!

Because there's hope now and an opportunity to actually meet our birth family, I've begun imagining the reunion. I've never done something so outrageous before . . . . To actually meet members of my Korean family seems like a fantasy . . . . A dream. Even though I have everything a human being wants and consider myself lucky, something is missing. I'm not sure if it's due to not having a close relationship with my adoptive mother or being separated from my birth mother or not experiencing cultural identity, or not knowing my life's origin. Something is missing. But I don't dwell on it. Or have I? What are other adoptees thinking, wishing, dreaming? Or does it even matter?

I imagine that meeting our natural mother will be a copycat version of "The Swan," a reality television program where producers take a "nobody" and, after an extreme make-over, untangle her into a "somebody." Jenette and I will have to prepare for such an event, a fairy tale come true! I imagine how newsworthy the reunion will be. Major Korean newspapers will write headlines on their front page: "Twins Originally Found in Box Are Finally Claimed!" And "Long Lost Parents Finally Find Their Beautiful Daughters!"

Jenette and I will have to spend hours preparing for our reunion in a closed room. Korean experts specializing in the styles best suited for us will choose classy outfits from famous designers. We'll have to try on many dresses to find our favorite one in my made-up vision, of course. The best cosmetologists will apply our make-up, and hairdressers will know which products to use to hold our thick hair in elegant updos for this event. They'll even find sparkling tiaras to crown us with, same as the popular beauty pageants I've seen. In my dreamy reunion, my birth family will be sweating in the front room, having no idea what to expect, wondering who we most resemble. Everyone will be anxiously sipping green tea to calm nerves, anticipating the moment of the "Big Reveal" just like on "The Swan" reality show. Soon it will come time for the lights to dim.

Not long ago, I had even consulted a Tarot Card Web site, typing from the keyboard: *will I find my birth family?* Dorothy and the "Wizard of Oz" card appeared on my computer screen:

When Dorothy appears in your reading, follow your destiny and proceed on your life quest . . . . Remain open to the entire range of possible destinations . . . . Eliminate the fear of getting lost and making mistakes . . . .

Hmm. Seems applicable. My mind jumps into the childish fairy tale reunion. We'll be surrounded by the media. The crowd hushes when it's time for the moment of truth. A spotlight flashes on. We face our Korean parents for the first time. *Omma* or mommy will recognize us immediately. *Ahboh* or Daddy will cry at the sight of us. A magical glow surrounds the four of us. In them, I see a reflection of me or who I could be. There's a weird knowingness in the air. Just by the gut, we understand both of them. We may even laugh the same way. Jenette and I can finally be ourselves . . . . Free to embrace, similar to any other family. Our Korean parents will then push us to the trembling arms of extended family—people who resemble us. For the first time in our lives, we won't be the minority. For the first time in our lives, we won't be so obviously different. At last, Jenette and I won't be the odd ones out. New relationships develop with relatives who remind Jenette and me of ourselves—no longer hidden; no longer are we lost from them. The honeymoon begins.

Snap. Blackness. A void. I rebuke myself for fantasizing. *Okay. I know. I should know better. I should know better! The fairy-tale is a little ridiculous.* I'm asking for way too much. I don't even know if I'm allowed to ever meet my family. I need to get my head out of the ground! I remind myself that I should know better. Adoption agencies warn adoptees against looking for our Korean parents, saying they might not want to meet us. I should stop daydreaming and stay focused on reality. I scold myself: *Stay focused on reality. Stay focused on reality. Stay focused on reality. Damn it, Janine! Stay focused!*

Good News

There are only two mistakes one can make along the road to truth; not going all the way and not starting.
—Buddha

We're going to celebrate adoption! I have to call my twin and tell her the good news! What's it like to be a twin? We pretty much agree on almost everything. Somehow, and for an unknown reason, we come to a consensus on virtually every topic. Maybe we've just learned how to cooperate at an early age, or maybe our "oneness" comes naturally. That doesn't mean we're not different. We lead diverse lives, and we are two completely separate people. I don't always agree with my sister's decisions, just as she doesn't agree with mine, but we still have lots of admiration for each other.

Jenette is not only business-oriented, but she's also thoughtful. Her business sense has helped her when contracting jobs and her natural ability to understand where people are coming from helps her to compassionately work with patients inside nursing homes. When I go to her work, she impresses me more than she knows. She has a comfortable rapport with the public—and she is especially drawn to the elderly. She tells me their lives are fascinating! I think that's the Gemini in us—life captivates us! When Jenette enters a hospital room, the energy literally rises to a higher level. My sister has an uncanny ability to uplift the patients due to being able to see the best in them. I'm referring to seeing past their limitations and into their soul.

Once, Jenette invited me to her work to visit one of her favorite bedridden patients. She needed only to stand by the woman's bedside, and it seemed as if the patient came alive with joy. It was like magic. I could see that my twin absolutely adored this woman, and she passed loving energy to her with affectionate eyes. After a few moments, the woman asked, "Jenette? Is God as nice as you? I hope God is as nice as you."

In contrast, I doubt I could work so affectionately in a nursing home environment. Hearing the stories where accidents have literally happened on my twin makes me nervous at the thought. But my sister takes each incident with a grain of salt. Jenette has also strained her back on more than one occasion when helping residents with their therapy, but she comes home optimistic. She believes every single one of them has a fascinating tale to tell. She can see into humanity's hearts and souls. Because we're twins, I get to live vicariously through her.

The strange thing is, during our thirty-two years together, the topic of our Korean family hadn't come up. Searching for them will interrupt our aspirations, but who knows what life has planned for us. Maybe it's time. What a fluke!

I fumble for my cell phone and push one of the pre-programmed buttons. It rings a few times before my twin answers.

"Yeah," she says, already knowing it's me.

"Jenette! You will never guess what I did today."

"What?" She whispers. "I have to talk quietly. I'm waiting for a patient right now."

I can't help but shout the good news. "I just went to the Korean newspaper!"

"You did?"

"Yeah. They were really nice," I say, still a little surprised. I half expected them to routinely kick me out. "They even helped me contact Holt's adoption agency in Seoul. They're helping us to find our birth parents!"

My thirty-two-year-old sister emphasizes each word. "Oh. My. God." Then she squeals like a pre-teen.

"I know. Isn't it amazing? We might actually meet our Korean parents!"

"Oh, my God. We have to meet for lunch. Let's meet at Ly's in an hour. This is amazing. I can't wait for the trip."

"Okay." My heart swells at the prospect. "The trip is gonna be great!"

"What if we find them?" My sister asks, attempting to be discreet around the therapists and residents working in clusters next to her.

"I know. It's gonna be weird."

"I wonder what they look like."

"I know," I say, stopping to imagine. "Remember what that psychic said? You look like dad; I look like mom."

"I know. It's gonna be so cool!"

I squeal. "I know!"

"I can't even imagine it!"

Hightailing out of the newspaper parking lot, I shout into the phone, "Okay. I'll meet you at Ly's in an hour!"

"Okay! I gotta go." She hangs up without saying bye.

An hour later, I lurk inside my Cambodian-born girlfriend's restaurant for lunch and scan dark candle-lit seating areas for my twin. I spot her in a solid, hand-carved elephant teak chair near the bar. She waves at me from a small round table next to the taupe-tiled fireplace. It's almost as if seeing my reflection in the mirror. Now that we're older, many barely know we're twins; as children, we looked so identical that I still can't tell us apart in old photos. We've been trying to look like two separate individuals since I can remember.

Both of us became young mothers with two children while in our early twenties. My sister has a thirteen-year-old son and a four-year-old daughter. I have two daughters, ages eleven and eight. We can't imagine life without them. It was scary at first, when the children were young, to manage work and care for them. But we've been fortunate. A Vietnamese woman and her two adult sons immigrated to the United States a month after my sister had her first child. The woman, Ba Bay, and her two adult sons needed help adjusting to the community, not knowing English fluently. They had been originally sponsored through a church by a fellow neighbor, who had more on his mind than he originally let on. He was hustling for a wife—or at least someone to clean his apartment and prepare his meals.

I remember the first time I had met Ba Bay and her sons, both close to my age. Her older son was full Vietnamese, and her younger son had the skin of a full-blooded African. He was actually Vietnamese. His father had been an African American soldier during the Vietnam War. I remember overhearing him speak Vietnamese on Jenette's phone, and, not knowing that he had any Asian blood in him, I gaped mystified at the "black" guy chattering away in a foreign language. It was so cool, and I was immediately drawn to the family.

Against the sponsoring neighbor's wishes, Jenette's Vietnamese boyfriend at the time drove Ba Bay and her sons to Seattle's International District, taught them how to open a bank account, filled out any necessary paperwork, and anchored them with traditional and the latest music and movies from back home. Feeling at ease with my sister and her boyfriend, the Vietnamese mother and sons frequented their apartment. As a result, Ba Bay's sponsor kicked the trio out of his one-bedroom apartment for not fulfilling their "obligations." Upon this traumatic event, Jenette and her boyfriend helped Ba Bay secure an apartment, and in return, the woman babysat for them and then for my husband and me when we had our daughters. A win-win for all involved; we have an affectionate appreciation for each other. Our children had been lavished with lots of grandmotherly love when we were working mothers in our twenties. Ba Bay could easily pull the four of us along with our children into her apartment, ladling out large bowls of Pho Ga (chicken soup), Bun Suong (Saigon noodle soup), Bun Bo Hue (beef noodle soup), or Mi Nuoc and Hai San (shrimp and crab noodle soup). Most westerners perceive cooking as a subservient task, but not Ba Bay. She fired up Vietnamese dishes proudly, exuding love and appreciation for us and empowered while doing so.

Even though Ba Bay isn't Korean, Jenette and I think of her as our "second" mother—that is, after our adoptive mom. We've never obsessed over our Korean mother, even as children. Out of honor for our adoptive parents, who have always been considered our "real" parents, birth parents do not deserve to be thought about, at least in adoptionland. Adopted people are expected to be satisfied with the family the agency matched us to. We've always honored our "swan" parents since they "really" did change our diapers and pay for our clothing and food. Our birth mother merely gave birth to us. Honoring mere biological strangers disrespects everything our adoptive parents did and sacrificed for us, according to Western Society.

Once seated in the traditional sturdy chair from Thailand, my sister jabs my arm. "Geez, it's going to be neat to meet other adoptees. You know, we've only known two others."

I nod, recalling the Korean faces of a friend in high school and my sister's old coworker. I liked them. They trudged through life, sometimes sarcastically, same as Jenette and me. "I wonder what happened to them."

"I mean, back then, we never talked about adoption." Jenette pulls smooth, shoulder-length hair behind her. "It was never considered a big deal."

"Yeah. That's right. That is weird. It'll be interesting to hear from them and those sent to Europe. Did you know adoptees flown to fifteen countries are supposed to be coming together for this event? Can you imagine?"

"We've just been so busy," my sister says, slurping a fancy iced coffee mocha through a clear straw. "We've never had the opportunity to hear what others have to say."

"It's probably cuz we've always had each other," I say, caressing my own iced Thai tea. "If we were adopted separately, we'd probably be more involved. We'd probably look into our backgrounds at a younger age."

It'll be strange to meet our family and to see them in us and us in them. "The Gathering," celebrating 50 years of overseas adoption, will be the first vacation out of the country Jenette and I will take alone. The possibilities excite us. With hopes of a successful reunion, I can't believe it's taken so long for Jenette and me to make this trip. As we dwell upon the idea of going to Korea, a deeper curiosity for my roots emerges. Of course, I appreciate my American family, but I still wonder if it's too late to find shoes that will fit our own feet. Will we find our own shoes? Is it fair to our parents to think solely about ourselves? Will we walk home with a fresh sense of confidence?

Change is a Constant

*Our greatest glory is not in never falling,
but in rising every time we fall.*
—Confucius

"So, Dad, Umm. Uh, what do you think about Jenette and me going to Korea?" I ask without thinking.

Dad smiles. "I think it's great. Did you know I took two hundred trips for Boeing?" He staggers along the neighborhood cul-de-sac, pushing a Rollator—an updated dark-blue four-wheeled walker for balance. Dad's hair has turned completely white, emphasizing intense green eyes. As he grasps the handles for balance, he slouches so that even though I'm only five feet tall, we're practically at eye level. Our journey together has been long. When I was growing up in the 1970s to the early eighties, Dad was a perfect swan. He was a Christian teacher, elder, youth group leader, choir director, and Boy Scout leader for a small community church. He preached the moral values of yesterday, where followers lived toward a vision of success and problems got solved in a day's episode. You can't get any more glorious than that.

That is until Dad reached the age of fifty-four when he began to hang glide. On October 20, 1984, he unintentionally "flew the coop." His life changed for the worse—or for the better—depending on how one chooses to look at it. On his seventh high-altitude flight, the glider folded during mid-flight, causing him to fall 100 feet through a tree, hitting his head several times on the branches. Thus began his life as a "disabled" person. He was forced to retire early from his engineering job, where he was employed for thirty-two years. Due to his newly inflicted disability, his schedule was reduced to mainly reading and watching television while confined to a recliner. His motto went from "Don't just sit there. Do something" to "Don't just do something. Sit there."

From the age of twelve, my twin and I have been emotionally supporting Dad throughout his recovery, providing care as he learned to adapt and accept his new physical limitations. We figure that if our family can overcome such a large life bump, we can pretty much overcome anything. Although Dad isn't entirely independent after his injury, his mind and heart are in sync, and he listens to issues of mine without brawls or snarls.

"Umm. Uh, Dad? Uh, what do you think . . . ." Trudging beside him on the South Seattle cement, I study him, not knowing how to ask the question without putting it bluntly. "What do you think about Jenette and me finding our birth parents?" It's a topic we've never discussed.

"What?"

"What do you think," I ask, now shouting, "about us finding our birth parents?"

His smile collapses, and he jerks and jiggles the Rollator to a stop, almost losing his balance. "I don't like it."

I'm surprised by his quick response. "Why?" I ask. By this time in our lives, I thought my sister and I had demonstrated our loyalties to him, and so, I hoped, he wouldn't think we were going to abandon him.

He's silent for a moment and then shakes his head. "I just don't."

"Can you give me a reason?"

"I don't like it." He rolls again. "I'm your father."

"Yeah. I can understand your feelings. I mean . . . I know I wouldn't be able to talk to Mom about this if she was still alive. But I always thought you were so much more open-minded."

"You're right, Janine." Dad's light ivory face stiffens, and forehead creases appear. "She wouldn't like it either."

"There's no way I could look for my birth parents if Mom was still around," I stutter, suddenly feeling childish. "Or, at least, I'd have to keep it a secret. And I would feel guilty too. But now it's the Gathering in Seoul. Adoptees from around the world are coming together for the 50-year reunion of overseas adoption. Our birth parents might be looking for us."

Dad lurches to another gallant stop. "I'm your father," he says, then starts rolling again.

I watch him push the Rollator around—each step choppy. He's seventy-three, but I've been told he could pass in age from anywhere between sixty to eighty years old. I think it's because of his injury.

Long ago, before Dad's injury, he was robust and forthright. He's probably the only person I know of who had the audacity to chase a state cop down a street for close to a mile because the officer pulled out in front of my parents and, as Dad tells the story with a laugh, "forced me to skid and veer to the next lane. The cop was totally in the wrong! He almost caused an accident, and it would have been his fault! If I had a ticket book, I'd slap him with a ticket!" This type of self-righteousness, blended with a hearty sense of humor over the cop's immediate apology, is the kind of person Dad used to be. If someone did something wrong—according to the rules belonging to the "Top Swan," Dad was determined to call the individual on his mistake and make him pay. My parents were good old-fashioned right-winged swans intent on flying the "right" way! The type of folks who fluffed their feathers at a

Billy Graham revival meeting and crooned bestowing all power to the "Great Big Bird," then went home and pecked at their ugly ducklings for veering off course during the hour-long lecture while at the same time calling us *lucky*.

The afternoon breeze rustles Dad's loose-fitting red T-shirt and Navy sweatpants as he circles the cul-de-sac at a snail's pace. Going around and around seems to reflect our lives together. Life appears to have always revolved around him. It's not easy to fly away when I see that's he's been grounded for the most part. Our family now laughs a lot. I enjoy being there for him, just as he's been around for me.

Dad's statement echoes in my mind, *I'm your father*.

I nod and nudge his elbow. "You'll always be my Dad. No matter what. But don't you think? Don't you think that the Korean population? When they hear what a great father you've been. How open-minded you are. Don't you think they'll find honor in that? Don't you think you'll get respect for that?"

Dad digests my words as he continues to push his Rollator along the sidewalk. Giant houses in the latest Pacific Northwest colors of rust, cocoa, evergreen, and sunflower gaze down at us. Wobbling ahead, he focuses on a bumper sticker on the wheeled walker. It was a Father's Day gift Jenette bought at the Boeing Museum of Flight that reads: "I'd rather be flying." For thirty-two years, he had been employed as a Boeing mechanical engineer, working on satellites, airplanes, the secretive "black box," and other projects he's kept private. After his injury, that part of his life came to a shocking halt, prompting twenty years of searching for the way out of suffering, which led to a move beyond Christianity and an expansion of awareness that includes world religions and spirituality.

"Don't you think our birth parents will be grateful? And who knows?" I shrug. "Maybe we can even take you to Korea so you can meet them."

"Oh, no." Dad grimaces. "I don't want to go to Korea. I should stay in America. Nothing beats the United States."

My parents have always been proud to be Americans, and with that came the impression that South Korea was a horrible country—a place that would have treated Jenette and me with disdain. Korea is a place where we would have either starved to death or become prostitutes. No one even needed to say this verbally—although the implication has been made. It was felt in the air by our parents' unintentional arrogance. Their disregard for other flocks, when we were kids, implied that we should deny our heritage and never consider making a voyage to such foreign soil. It's been my curiosity that makes the trip more appealing rather than appalling as Dad sees it.

If I were any younger, I wouldn't go; just the thought might have seriously jeopardized my relationship with my parents. To think that I belong to another flock—a Korean family—would have caused my adoptive parents to feel bad, risking potential pain for everyone involved. I can't even imagine bringing up the topic of other parents around my late adoptive mother. Our relationship as a "real" mother and daughter could have been questioned. Nope. Out of respect for my adoptive mother, I wouldn't take the risk if she was still alive. Doing a search would be a serious violation and dishonor for all Mom did for us. I would hate to jeopardize our relationship by following up on my own curiosity.

I nudge Dad's arm, a little disappointed that he is so afraid of what I'll find. It's not my intention to replace him if that's what he thinks. "Don't you think Mom understands now?" Trying to make him feel better. "She's probably watching us from heaven. I'm sure she's cheering for us."

"What?" My dad hollers without realizing our neighbors can probably hear our conversation.

"Mom understands now," I say discreetly.

"What?" Dad blares.

"Now that Mom is in heaven, she sees us from a more loving perspective. She understands!" Embarrassed, I scan the neighborhood, hoping no one is listening.

Dad nods but doesn't say anything, and we continue to walk in large cul de sac circles. I assure myself that going will be the right thing. My husband had told me that he plans to take care of Dad, the kids (including Jenette's two), the house, and the dog. "I think it's time," he had said even though he worried for me. "You should go. Don't worry. I've got everything under control." He had also encouraged me years back to become a U.S. citizen when I found out upon Mom's death that my parents never applied for Jenette and my citizenship—it wasn't required upon adopting us. According to documents, we were still "alien immigrants" and foreign children—floaters between two nations. Throughout my twenties, I had been more loyal to Dad than to myself. Now, in my early thirties with my own family, it might be time to consider my own past, at last.

As I round another circle with Dad, I promise myself that I will definitely make the trip with Jenette even though he is a bit unsettled at the thought. I enter the house through the garage door while he turns away from me to open the side gate, a route with fewer bumps and barriers. Upon taking our separate routes to get inside, Dad shouts one of his most popular words of wisdom, "One thing is for sure, Janine. Change is the only constant in life."

Crossing Boundaries

*A Zen monk is a concentration of energy
that is available immediately for anything.*
—D.T. Suzuki

At SeaTac Airport, Jenette and I meet several adoptees from the Seattle area who are boarding the same plane this Saturday afternoon. Upon numerous introductions, I can already identify with the group's easy-going aura. There's an unspoken kinship even though we're strangers. To suddenly be in the majority is rare. When I was a child, it was somewhat shocking to see birds with features and feathers like mine. Fortunately, the Pacific Northwest has finally blossomed multi-ethnic colors. I still feel like a separate species when face to face with "real" Koreans, especially since I do not speak my "mother" tongue. There is usually a gap wherever Jenette and I go. But not here! And not now!

At the boarding gate, we have hours before it's time to leave. I decided to peruse the shops, buy snacks and magazines before embarking. At the Starbucks line, I see my twin race over to me, dragging a small rolling suitcase behind with two smaller bags wrapped around her. She's wearing a short denim jacket and khakis and could pass for a schoolgirl. Once she reaches the line, it's hard to stop. She crashes into me, almost knocking my own bundles out of order.

"I've met a twin," she pants.

"Cool."

"He's in the medical field—just like me!"

"Hey, that's awesome."

"Only he's w-a-a-y smarter!—He's a doctor."

"Oh, my gosh."

"But you'd never think he was a doctor, cuz he's so laid back! Not authoritative or scientific. He seems like a really nice guy. And he's tall!"

"How tall?"

He's, like, six feet tall!"

"Wow."

"And he's got a twin!"

"What's his twin like?"

"A female."

"A female?"

"Yeah. She lives in another state. She's going to be at the conference. I can't wait to meet her!"

The rushed cashier fills my order of two grande double-shot skinny iced mocha lattes with no whip. Jenette and I stroll back to the waiting area, hugging our various bags and cold drinks. It's going to be a long trip. Adoptees linger around the terminal, snacking and purchasing reading material from the gift shops near the boarding gate. I hope that the flight to "motherland" will satisfy my natural wonder regarding identity and self. I think it's natural to feel an innate need to reconnect with one's birthplace. There's another reason. I've heard that "people want to know their roots so they can fly." We're pulling back time so we can spring forward. As adoptees, we're caught in the middle—curious about the flock we most resemble but becoming family with the "unknown" coop the stork had taken us to years back.

Jenette and I have wandered in separate directions by the time the announcement for boarding has been called. I'm not too worried since I know we'll be sitting next to each other on the airplane. When I'm in line for boarding, my twin taps me from behind. This time, her arm is linked with a gal we had met three months prior.

"I adopted a li'l sis," Jenette shares. "Remember Christina?"

Christina giggles, and then the two of them exchange glances. *Yep. She's definitely a Seoul sister!* She has the same shaped eyes, the color of sea beans, the same latte-colored skin, the same soft black-brown hair as Jenette and me. My twin and her new younger friend burst into identical contagious laughs. Yes, I remember meeting the teen from the 2004 Rainbow Bookfest. I was sitting in the middle of the Seattle Union Station on one of the panel discussions, waiting for a question from an audience member regarding a book I had written. Local authors shared the microphone at a long table inside the 1600 square foot brick Great Hall, and voices echoed off the walls. I could overhear my sister and her new friend joke and hoot from behind our small audience. My twin and her new friend were even playfully teasing each other, then laughing hysterically like BFFs (Best Friends Forever) as if they had known each other for thousands of years.

Later I learned that Christina had read my book. (*So she was the one!*) While I was on the panel, she had approached Jenette, totally serious, and given her a series of compliments. My twin, loving every moment of it, waited until the teen was done before finally admitting, "Okay. That's great. But I didn't write the book." Jenette pointed to me sitting at the panel (staring back at them) and laughed, "She did. Now, say the same thing. Only say it to her!" Both of them shrieked in laughter. By the time I approached them, Christina and Jenette had linked arms, and they were jumping around like long lost but finally found sisters, blaring, "Oh, my Gawd! You're going to the Gathering? Oh, my Gawd! I'm going to the Gathering!"

During the flight, I close my eyes and imagine South Korea. Seoul is fast becoming a reality. Visiting the street corner where we had been abandoned, the orphanage, and the police station seems amazingly possible. Jenette and I can't wait to be there. On a once-in-a-lifetime trip, we plan to take as many photos as possible. I assume because we are twins that we will find our family easily, and I wonder how emotional the reunion will be. My soul tingles. Then, I try to suppress the thought so I won't be disappointed if it doesn't happen. Jenette and I banter back and forth on everything we should do while there. We know the priority, though, which is to find our Korean family, the missing link.

What do we want to do while in Korea? The place our adoptive parents believed to be a backward country. Their hallway shelves used to store books written by Christians that portrayed the South Korean blue and red emblem as "evil" and even demonic. I can't believe the shopping districts are open until five in the morning. I'm fascinated by the travel brochures. They make Seoul look so modernized and hip while at the same time depict ancient and traditional parts of the culture inside and outside the city. We've been told to be careful—hold onto our belongings, keep purses and bags close under our arms, be wary of everyone, especially strangers acting in peculiar ways, keep everything in sight, try not to let anyone know you're a foreigner. Try not to look like a foreigner. Blend in.

I pull out a small orange guidebook from the Korea National Tourism Organization and study its pages. Maybe I can learn a few Korean words! Flipping through it, I find the pages showcasing a few Korean passages along with the English translation. I try to sound out each word yet feel embarrassed while doing so—as if a preschooler. Am I even close to pronouncing the words, right? Each word is long and lingering.

"Geez, Jenette. Look at these words." I pass her the travel booklet and point to a few basic phrases: *cheo-eum boepgetseoyo* (how do you do?), *mannaseo bangawoyo* (I'm glad to meet you), *eodiseo taeksireul talsu isseulkkay?* (Where can I get a taxi?), and *geuguoseun eolma-imnikka?* (How much is it?).

Jenette grabs the book from me and stares. "What the heck? Why are the words so long?"

"How are we going to communicate?" I ask, self-doubt growing. I attempt to sound out the word *sillye-hamnida* (excuse me), but I don't even know if I'm pronouncing it correctly. "We'll never learn the language. We're going to look so retarded."

Jenette laughs, studying the text in the back of the silent and darkened airplane. "Man, these are the longest words I've ever seen."

"I know! Thank God we're going in a group." When I look over the passages, I feel overwhelmed. Words stick in my throat, and my tongue twists into a pretzel.

"It's better not to think about it," Jenette says, shoving the tiny book back into my hands.

"Yeah." I agree and shove the book into my bag. "I bet the Koreans speak English over there, anyway," I say, somewhat relieved.

"Yeah. Almost everyone speaks English. Thank God!"

"There's so much to do! Palaces. Temples. And royal tombs!"

"Yeah. I'm glad we're going together." Jenette sighs.

"Yeah. Can you imagine trying to make the trip alone?"

Jenette laughs in a whisper. "We're going to look a lot like idiots to the real Koreans."

"Yeah. And dummies," I add.

The two of us burst into laughter, much like identical stereo speakers. We cover our mouths and slouch into the cramped seats, attempting to muffle our glee.

"Yeah, Janine. We've been waiting for this trip forever!"

"Yeah, I know," I say. "It's a trip of a lifetime!"

Shooting Blanks 2003

How simple a thing it seems to me that to know ourselves as we are, we must know our mothers' names.
—Alice Walker, O Magazine, May 2003

It'll take at least eleven hours to get to Seoul. After skimming books and magazines, watching a movie, and listening to music, my mind slips to the nearby past. My origin, my history, and my lineage seem more of a mystery than ever now that my attention is focused on me. *Do I have blood ties? Do I have a Seoul family?*

Sometimes Jenette and I are at a loss for words when someone meets us and asks: "which is the older twin?" We usually shrug, or if we decide to be funny, both will point to ourselves and then, as if on cue, point to each other. Eventually, we're forced to tell the truth: we don't know. Our adoption documents don't tell.

At our adopted mother's death, I started writing a book based on Dad's disability and recovery and ended up self-publishing it after three years of ranting and raving over what I should do with it. Based on my lack of knowledge, I titled my memoir akin to a newspaper headline. Since we can remember, my twin and I were told we had been found in a box on a Seoul street corner, so *Found in a Box* sprouted into my mind. The title seemed appropriate. We were literally and figuratively "found in a box!"

I hadn't really thought that my adoption could be a big deal—or maybe I just didn't want to make it a big deal. Why make mountains out of molehills? Because of the memoir I had written with the subtitle: *Adapting to Adoption*, one might assume I had researched adoption back then. I hadn't. Nothing and no one in my life could make me think that my adoption mattered. The intention behind writing my book was to share *Dad's* story, his tenacity, and *his* courage caused by *his* hang gliding injury. I never questioned his status as my father, and the book was not supposed to be a reflection of my life!

When I finished proofreading, my editor, a mother of two biological daughters, told me, "You know, throughout your book, you were really adapting to your adoption."

I shook my head 'no' without thinking. "I was?" The idea shocked me. "No, see, my adoptive parents are my 'real' parents. Didn't I make that clear?" *Adoption could never be the problem. The problem was me. No. Nothing in my life has to do with my adoption. No one has a bonding mother-daughter relationship. Mother and daughters aren't supposed to get along—especially during the teenage years. Mothers are supposed to be agitated and annoyed by their daughters.*

The editor suggested the book be subtitled "*Adapting to Adoption.*" I hadn't ever thought that a disconnection could have anything to do with my adoption. Wasn't my childhood pretty normal? All-American? As far as I was concerned, Dad was my "real" Dad; Mom, my "real" Mom.

Because of the book, I was invited to participate in various book fests. One of which was Seattle's Rainbow Bookfest put together by a woman from the Northwest Asian Weekly and many volunteers. During one of my first showings at the festival in 2003, people involved with adoption asked, "Where have you been? You've popped up from nowhere!"

As each individual dawdled past our table, they gave us bits and pieces of information regarding something called a "Gathering." This event was supposed to happen the following year, August 2004. According to an article published in 1999 by the Korean newspaper, *Korea Herald*, at least 2000 Korean-born adoptees visit Korea each year in search of their national, cultural, ethnic, or biological heritage. Seoul seemed appropriate to host the third International "union" of Korean-born adoptees. There had only been two international gatherings in previous years. The first one was held in Washington, DC, in 1999. The second conference took place in Oslo, Norway, in 2001. Jenette and I missed both—hadn't heard of the events. In both Gatherings, Korean-born adoptees were given the opportunity to meet, share, and network with adoptees, many for the first time. Workshops and exhibits on adoption, culture, and ethnicity were presented. Boy, have Jenette and I been out of the loop!

When I shared my story with bookfest participants, questions concerning my adoption became harder to answer, and I was forced to actually reflect upon the status of my birth. *How was I adopted? Why was I adopted? Exactly where was I found? Who found me?* Just a year prior, when a producer from a Seattle studio gave me a pre-television interview, I had trouble answering her, responding to her inquiry on my origin with self-doubt due to knowing close to nothing. Zero. Zilch.

The pre-show interview with the producer, intended to see if my story was "big" enough to air on her live television show, went, in my view, awkwardly. I had hoped that my failure to give totally confident answers might force her to deny me from being on her show. Now that I look back, the pre-show interview over the telephone was pretty funny:

The producer, on the phone, asked for factoids, hoping to find snippets of newsworthy information. She first asked, "What's your first memory?"

Holding the phone with my shoulder, I remembered darting into Dad's room just in case he could answer the questions more accurately for me. I knew nothing—a blank slate. I paced, staring into Dad's green eyes while stuttering into the phone: "Well . . . Um . . . I remember being in a crib at my parents' home."

"Were you with your adopted family or birth family?" She inquired.

"I was with my adopted family. I remember . . . Jenette . . . in a crib next to mine." *What a stupid answer!* My mind raced over visuals . . . Anything just to get words to leave my mouth, searching for a memory. *The crib in Mom and Dad's room. Stuff. Boxes. Stuff-filled boxes. Boxes filled with stuff. Nothing that seems significant. Darkness when thinking of Korea—nothing reflecting Korea at all.*

"So you were found in a box?"

Scared speechless and watching Dad lounge in his lazy blue chair, I replied, "Yes." My fingers clenched the phone. *He's the one who should answer these questions!*

"Tell me about it."

"Well, there's really not much to tell."

"Was the lid on it?"

"Umm. I don't know."

"Were there blankets?"

Covering the mouthpiece, I repeated the question to Dad, but he only shrugged, not helping. His inability to give answers slightly bothered me. According to him, it was a frivolous matter. Why waste time talking about it? We were his daughters. End of story. It was impossible to stay mad at my father for his happy-go-lucky attitude. Before this, I didn't even bother to wonder as if my Korean family and my own ethnic heritage simply did not exist. In fact, if someone were to tell me that I was "Korean," I'd surely deny it! *How offensive!* By habit, I'd demand, "No. I'm American!"

Over the phone, I stuttered, "We don't. We don't have. We don't have the police record . . . So we don't know." I felt so ridiculous for not being able to give more confident answers.

"Paint me a picture. Show me what happened," the producer pushed. "Give me a scene. Where were you found?"
"On a street corner." *(At least that's what I've been told)*
"What country?"
"Korea."
"North or South?"
"South."
"Do you know what city?"
"Seoul."
"Were you just born or a few months old?"

Covering the mouthpiece again, I hissed at my father for knowing so little. "Dad, do you know how old we were when we were found?"

Tight-faced, he shrugged, giving the television show *Little House on the Prairie* more attention than me.

"No," I said, uncomfortable.
"Who found you?"
"We don't know."
"Can you give me some of your history?"
"I don't. I don't know," I replied, realizing how strange I probably sounded. I had written a book but still didn't know my life's basics.

"Okay, you've got to expand," the producer urged. "Give me more than one-word answers. Paint me a picture. Say, 'my twin and I were found on a street corner in Seoul, Korea, 1972. A stranger heard our cries and delivered us to the nearby police station.'"

"Okay." But the sentences would be hard to say. They seemed so recorded—so fake—didn't seem true to me. How could I lie? How could I talk about my birth without proof?

"Do you have photos of yourself as an infant?"

I thought for a while. I remembered seeing one, but I didn't know where it went. The answer was "No."

After Mom had died, we did receive a few papers. But, she was adamant that we stay away from her possessions. Our childhood home was filled to the max with boxes, and that is the second reason I used *"Found in a Box"* for the title of my book.

"Was it by accident that you have no photos?"

"Probably by accident. But it could also have been on purpose."

"Do you have any photos of yourself while in Korea?"

"Umm. No."

"You mean you don't have infant photos?"

"Umm. No."

"Do you have any photos of your birth family?"

"Umm. No," I paused, growing more irritated with myself over this interrogation.

"A letter from your birth family?"

"Umm. No."

"Anything from your birth family? Maybe left hidden down in the box you were found in?"

"Not as far as I know."

"Relatives from Korea?"

"Umm. Not that I know of."

Boy, did I feel like an idiot? I didn't know anything about Korea! I didn't speak Korean. I didn't know how to cook Korean food. I didn't even know what they ate. What are their holidays? Was I born in the city or the country or by the East Sea? What time was I born? Did I resemble my natural father or mother? Which of their mannerisms and/or demeanor did I take after? Who were my extended family members, and do I resemble them? Did I have brothers, sisters, aunts, uncles, cousins, nieces, or nephews? What was the health history of my family tree? What did my family do for work or play? Did they follow Taoism? Buddhism? Christianity? Did they ever wonder about Jenette and me?

Unaware of the uncertainty building within me triggered by what felt akin to the television producer's nagging questions, she continued to ask me more as if this issue was so easy to answer:

"Were you given letters from the adoption agency?" She asked.

"Umm. Not that I know of."

"You mean, absolutely no correspondence?"

"Umm," I said, realizing that since my adoption, I've been living my life totally blank. "Umm. Not that I know of."

Traveling through life as an adoptee was close to trying to walk in shoes too big. It was nearly impossible to walk with confidence. How do I narrate my history with so much uncertainty? Did other adoptees have the same sick sense? I was so unsure of myself—my shoes didn't fit. How was I to wear them, walk my talk and talk my walk? How was I to walk confidently in shoes too big?

After an hour and a half of curious questions met with doubtful two- or three-word sentences and short answers, we reached the end of the telephone conversation with dull silence.

My heart raced. *Umm. Damn. I feel like such an idiot!*

The producer requested to talk with Dad, attempting to retrieve history from him. Between spaces of silence, Dad gave answers just as uncertain and terse as mine. Maybe he wanted to avoid talking about my adoption—something he didn't know much about either. And besides, Jenette and I belonged to him. We were *his* daughters. Dad changed the subject back to the defining moment in *his* own life—*his* hang gliding injury. He talked into the phone extra loud, unable to hear himself due to failing hearing aids: "I don't know. Did you know I wasn't even aware that this was going on? I simply don't remember my accident. Did you know I rode in a helicopter for the first time in my life, and I don't even remember it?"

I affectionately rolled my eyes at him, knowing he enjoyed being the center of attention. He bellowed into the phone: "I barely remember the last nineteen years. I don't remember much of my marriage, but I do remember my childhood in great detail. I lived on Sumner Street—"

I tapped my fingers impatiently while my father rambled on focusing on his own life. Unable to read my moans of worry, the conversation finally reverted back to the topic of our adoption. "I think the girls' mother has their records. No, you can't talk with her," Dad told the producer. "She's dead." He held the phone at me, unconcerned.

Pulling the phone from Dad's stiff fingers, I expected the producer to smirk and sting me with her decision to cancel our appearance on her program—in fact, I was hoping she would. How do we share life details with an interested audience when we didn't know the truth? Shockingly, she told me to get prepared—they plan to have Jenette and me on in a week. Our story *was* interesting. I swore at myself for being so stupid and perpetuating this interview, ready to rebuke myself for having the audacity to even consider discussing my origin when I knew nothing. Zip. Nada. My life should just be kept on the backburner. How do I discuss adoption when I didn't ever ask to know more? Friends tried to comfort me before the television interview. "The interview will be a breeze," they told me. "No one knows you better than yourself."

Fortunately, the interviewer grasped the obvious and avoided the topic of our adoption. Instead, she focused on our bizarre childhood—Dad's head injury and our beloved Mother's hoarding problem. Jenette and I whizzed through the hour show with no questions on our origin. Relieved, I thought, maybe we don't need to know. *It's really no big deal*, I eventually concluded.

First Supper

"The seemingly simple act of preparing food is an important cultural characteristic."
—Korean Food Guide

At last, we're here! Seoul, South Korea. By the time Jenette and I exit Asiana, our new Seattle friends are nowhere to be found. Big gulp. We're on our own! A gnawing feeling settles in my gut upon leaving Incheon Airport. I feel akin to a toddler without a grown-up to tell me what to do and where to go. The airport, one of Asia's most technologically advanced, seems so vast! It was even voted the world's best airport in service and quality by the International Air Transport Association (IATA) and Access Control Interface (ACI).[1] I can't help but notice the beauty in the modern glass architecture. It reminds me of the 1990 action-adventure science-fiction movie *Total Recall,* where the main character, played by Arnold Schwarzenegger, buys a "holiday" at Recall Inc. due to gnawing dreams reflecting a past life on Mars. The reality of his situation is constantly in question. Who is he? Which personality is correct? Which version of his reality is true? Those in control attempt to repress his true identity.

I can relate. Sometimes I wonder. *Who am I? Which personality is correct? Do I have any Korean in me?* I can't wait to find out about my past. With only half the day before conference registration, we have little time. My sis and I need to get to the hotel as soon as possible.

Only in the nineteenth century did Seoul open up to foreigners. An American by the name of Angus Hamilton visited the city in 1904 and said, "The streets of Seoul are magnificent, spacious, clean, admirably made and well-drained. The narrow, dirty lanes have been widened, gutters have been covered, roadways broadened. Seoul is within measurable distance of becoming the highest, most interesting, and cleanest city in the East."[2] Between 1910 and 1945, Japan occupied Korea. Then, in 1950, the Korean War broke out. Today, Seoul is considered one of the top 20 "world-class cities," affecting global affairs through socio-economic, cultural, and/or political means.[3]

I read in the guidebook that the location of Seoul was selected 600 years ago after careful consideration by King T'aejo, the founder of the Dynasty, using a method called geomancy. Geomancy, similar to feng shui, is the belief that the location of a site must be ideally placed to exert a lasting and decisive influence over the destinies of the occupants and family members. The basic theory of geomancy originated from the belief that the earth, being the mother and producer of all of life, exercises a decisive influence over those who utilize the land. Therefore, the location had to be carefully selected, first determining where the earth's energy was stored and then flowed.

From Incheon to Seoul, Jenette and I, along with many Korean passengers, travel by bus in the early evening over a skinny highway, past small rectangular cottages, swaying rice fields, and trees in the distance. Dark green hills roll into mountains with breathtaking peaks. We marvel at the scenery. The view of the rice paddies along the way soothes and calms our spirits, while air conditioning gives relief from the sizzling and sultry August conditions.

South Korea, a little smaller than Washington State, hangs below North Korea, which is bordered by China. Based on the little I heard from U.S. news reports, the people of South Korea are at risk of a potential attack from a much more controlling North Korean government. Families living in North and South Korea are kept separated by a carefully watched border. Seoul, the capital of South Korea, is the center of political, economic, and cultural activity known for serving as the gateway to the world.

Soon enough, the bus passes through high rises of cement, brick, and glass. The streets of Seoul resemble those of Seattle. Cars slip in and out of traffic, with drivers in a rush but more composed than Seattle drivers—or maybe it's just my receptive mood that casts a spell of meditative calm. Korean characters are splashed on fiberglass signboards in green, black, red, and white, reminding me how foreign I am. Run-down brick, cement, and wood structures badly in need of repair resemble Seattle's International District, where Asians from China, the Philippines, Vietnam, Cambodia, Thailand, and South Korea converge. Full-length shop windows showcase Western mannequins dressed in white wedding gowns. McDonald's, Starbucks, KFC, and Pizza Hut populate the streets. This city has Western influence written all over it. The downtown traffic reflects off tall glass buildings. Emotions stay confined within vehicles as drivers weave in and out, making quick decisions that cause narrow misses, close calls, and U-turns that barely miss pedestrians on narrow streets and alleys.

We arrive at the Sofitel Ambassador Hotel and find that it is one of the nicest buildings Jenette and I have ever stepped foot in. I did not know it had a five-star rating, catering specifically to business travelers. When we order a simple glass of fresh-squeezed orange juice, we're shocked to find out that a glass is eleven U.S. dollars. We were expecting third-world prices! Turns out, this place is more expensive than our hometown.

Once Jenette and I settle into our room, we scrounge around for a place to eat. Totally ravished, we explore each floor and each offering, feeling really "American" at the moment since those around us are "real" Koreans. We're happy that we at least know how to use chopsticks. We might look utterly silly if we, as adult female Koreans, do not even know how to use simple eating utensils!

There are six restaurants we can choose from, each providing more than we had expected. Through the glass windows, we see there's an ultra-modern bar embellished with flat white leather couches accented with red pillows on a sapphire carpet. Then there's a café of light snacks, a lounge and delicatessen, a first-class Chinese restaurant offering International Cuisine, and a Japanese restaurant. These locations flaunt traditional Asian décor and modern Western influence. Finally, when we land on the bottom floor, we notice an all-you-can-eat buffet shoved in the back corner.

A man in a navy blue suit and tie stands at a podium with a menu and smiles upon our arrival. With dark brown eyes, we watch him, and with the same dark brown eyes, he watches us, but we're unable to say much of anything. Jenette and I scan the menu, looking for the prices, feeling his eyes on our backs.

"Hmm. It's too pricey," I tell Jenette. After fumbling with the currency exchange in my mind, I guestimated that lunch might be around seventy U.S. dollars each—way more than we usually spend for a meal.

She nods in agreement but says without looking up from the menu, "He's cute. Look at his smile."

Ignoring her comment, I try to tell the man "too expensive" with a multitude of stupid hand motions.

He points us inside and nods his head yes, despite my hesitance.

I shake my head no, still a bit uneasy.

The man directs us to the dining room with the grace of the host from the 1970's *"The Price is Right"* game show. I'm resistant, however, afraid that we'd be spending a little too much money, especially for our first day. So I continue to shake my head no, unrelentingly.

That's when he gives us a peace sign, then points to the price, and then in a hushed voice, says something that appears to mean: "for one."

Jenette and I shrug and wonder. "What? What's he saying?"

The man continues to point to the price and then gives us the peace sign with a "one."

"What's he saying?" I ask.

"Oh, my God, Janine," Jenette tells me. She's been unintentionally flirting with him by twisting her long hair into knots with her fingers. She tugs my arm and pulls me inside the restaurant. "I think he's letting both of us in, and we only have to pay for one meal!"

"No way."

"Come on!" She shoves me inside.

The man turns around and leads us into the dining room, guiding us to a comfortable booth under a gigantic chandelier. Our heels click against the hardwood floor, and the view is a lap of luxury: long marble counters display everything from California rolls and shrimp with lemon and cocktail sauce plated on white ceramic to hot foods under silver domes, opened as if giant treasure chests.

"Oh, my God, Janine! This is like a Las Vegas buffet!" my sister screeches, throwing her bag into the booth set against traditional English paneling and then scooting in after it.

"Wow." I take in the view.

After filling our plates, the man ventures over with a Polaroid camera in hand. With more motions, he asks to take our photo. We nod and pose.

After he leaves, my sister swoons, "Boy, he's cute." She thrusts a tiny round kimbap (a Korean "sandwich" of rice wrapped in dried seaweed) into her mouth, somehow managing a smile at the same time.

I nod, peeling the pink shrimp open and heaving meat into my own wide grin.

As soon as we're done, we hold our tummies and dawdle around the hotel resembling two calm and collected penguins. Upstairs, Jenette peers through double doors.

"Oh, my God." My sister smirks. It's the room where the conference will take place, and the doors will be opened soon.

"What?" I ask.

"We're dorks," Jenette says.

"Why?"

"Look inside." My twin tells me, giving me room for a peek.

I glance inside and see another all-you-can-eat buffet is laid out on long display tables, revealing more silver treasure chests. "Oh, my gosh." I snicker, also holding my own gut. "We're idiots!"

When the doors open, we scout the buffet, but this time, we're hungry to get to know Korean adoptees sent overseas and around the world.

My sister jabs me. "Oh, look! There's doctor twin!" And she darts off.

Information Age

Self-reverence, self-knowledge, self-control—
These three alone lead to sovereign power.
—Alfred, Lord Tennyson

Sunlight streaming through the partially opened hotel curtains alert Jenette and me to get up. Barely rested, we are ready to explore the city early this morning. A swoosh reverberates through the room when I fling the red curtains open the rest of the way, revealing the eight-lane city street below.

This is going to be a good day. Quite possibly the best day of our lives! I'm not sure I've ever felt such euphoria in my life. In spite of my jubilation, one of Korea's characteristics I can't ignore is the tranquility that seems to exude from the city. It's so peaceful. I mean, it's not as if people whisper. I'm talking about energy. The energy is so soft and gentle, unlike the states. The diverse mixing of birds in the United States can sometimes feel as if each flock needs to prove that it's "acceptable" to other groups who have pre-conceived notions and assumptions about each flock. Here, there is no need to prove anything or to explain *me*.

I have the same feathers as everyone else. What an unfamiliar but comforting concept!

It's the first day of the conference and Jenette, and I have decided to skip the registration and opening ceremonies to scout out our life history. At the downstairs café, we sit at a table, next to the windows inside the delicatessen. My sister has a view of the lounge while I'm facing outside.

"Janine. Oh, my God. Don't look now," Jenette whispers without moving her lips, eyeing the back corner. "There are three guys over there, and they're staring at us."

I begin to turn around.

"Don't. Don't look," she reiterates, grabbing my arm, and then she pretends to look off to the side. "I'll tell you when to look."

While she stares in silence, gawking and fixing her hair with no success, I obey. "What do they look like?"

"They're Korean." She tells me without moving her mouth. "Oh, my gosh. They could be related to us." She realizes aloud. "Oh, my gosh. Anyone here could be a family member."

Oh my gosh. That means she can't date anyone here even if she wanted to.

"They're looking at us again." My twin says emotionless. "Okay. Now, slowly look back and pretend to look at the clock in the upper corner."

I obey her ridiculous commands, turning around as discreetly as possible, in search of the clock but really looking for the men. My sister can be such a dork at times. I spotted the three men in Cambridge shirts, and gray slacks, ranging in age from maybe late-thirties to mid-forties recline in chairs, drinking coffee, and looking right at us. Suit jackets, briefcases, and papers are strewn on the table. Their eyes are glued in our direction. I jerk back around and carp, "There is no clock. I feel like an idiot."

"They're still looking at us," she says through a smile, eyes pretending not to notice. "Oh, God. They just waved."

Unbelievingly, I watch my twin wave back and then leave her chair to meet them as if a smiling zombie before I can say anything to stop her.

Mumbling, I joke to myself after she leaves the table. "She better not get too serious with anyone of them. What if they're our long-lost Korean brothers?"

I watch my identical twin approach the group from a distance. They react surprised that she doesn't speak Korean. Previously, I didn't give it much thought, but, boy, we must look peculiar. We look Korean, but naive on the country and the language! The men start the conversation with a simple question. "Why don't you speak Korean?"

They speak English! I join my sister while she introduces herself and then starts in on our story. Since this is an international event planned by adult adoptees wearing the same shoes as we are, there are many professionals ready to help with language, like the two wealthy Korean associates we come to know as "Mr. Lee and his boss." Mr. Lee and his boss become sensitive to our plight and are inspired to help when Jenette expands upon our story, showing them the book I've written. They open cell phones to start the investigation we've been waiting so long for. Since Mr. Lee speaks English and Korean, he translates our wants to his associate.

We rattle off loudly when we tell our story to the two men as if they'll understand us better the louder we speak. We probably come across as pushy, but in the states, we've learned, sometimes the only way to be heard is to "raise the roof!"

"The street from your adoption document does not exist," Mr. Lee whispers while his associate dials numbers. "My boss is going to make another call."

Jenette and I sit quietly, attempting to eavesdrop even though there's no way we can understand Korean. To distract myself, I stare at the sparkling orange koi fish jet along the calm waters in a long cement pond. On the surface, I mirror their serenity; inside, I'm eager and energized, ready to jump out and explore this unknown land. We want a souvenir photo of three places: the street we were said to have been found on, the adoption agency, and the police station we were said to have been delivered to. First, we want to take a photo of the street, and then we plan to pick up birth records from the adoption agency.

Between calls, Mr. Lee updates us with his boss's status, trying to get bits of information according to the document we had from Holt. "Still, can't find the street." His eyes remain concerned. "It doesn't seem to exist."

I glance at my watch. He's been on the phone for twenty minutes trying to locate the street we were found on, according to the Holt Document from 1972. I listen as the men speak my mother tongue, wishing I could communicate and do the "dirty" work so I'd feel more in control. There's so much I want to say and add, but I can do nothing but listen to unfamiliar sounds. I watch in anticipation as Mr. Lee's boss dials numbers on his cell phone, nods, grunts, and looks toward Jenette and me, jotting more numbers on a scrap of paper.

Based on information from a police station, he tells us the street we were said to have been found on doesn't exist and, oddly, never did. Something is said in relation to the street names being changed throughout the years. The four of us agree, to get the truth, we must visit Holt Agency's Post Adoption Services building. Mr. Lee and his boss agree to assist us there.

Jenette and I ride in the backseat of a spotless black Cadillac. Mr. Lee needs to stop at several locations in Seoul before finding the correct office, which ends up being the Holt Reception Building. Inside the vehicle, Jenette and I get to sit on smooth russet leather seats, signifying affluence we did not expect to find in South Korea. Believing the rumors I had always heard in our adoptive country, I had expected the residents to be in poverty, dressed in hand-me-downs, with children begging for us to give them money on the street. But this is not the case. To my surprise, the residents are more technically advanced. Why hadn't anyone told me this? Seoul is as affluent as Seattle. Where are the begging street children we've heard so much about? It's really strange. The streets seem to be begging for children!

We arrive in an area of Seoul that does not consist of high rises and glass buildings. We don't say it, but when we peer through the back window, our hearts race at the sight of the brick Post Adoption Services building. This will be the pinnacle of the thirty-two years of our lives. *We've actually made it! We're actually at the Holt Children Services Post Adoption Reception Center. Amazing!*

The two Korean men open the back Cadillac doors and escort us to the front doors to the building, and then we're instructed by a woman to don guest slippers. After climbing a flight of cement stairs, the four of us reach a white-walled, square office, and the Korean men stand aside. A woman, close to my age, is sitting at her desk when we approach the counter.

"Do you have an appointment?" She asks, staring at a computer screen.

Surprised and relieved that she lacks a Korean accent, I answer eagerly, "No. But we did e-mail here a few times from Seattle via the Korea Post. We're here because of the 50-year anniversary Adoptee Gathering."

"You're supposed to have an appointment," she dryly says, without looking at us.

"We did try . . . To get into contact with this office . . . Before our trip," I stammered, caught off guard by her hostile welcome.

An announcement of the Adoptee Gathering scribbled in large letters with thick red ink on a whiteboard behind her excites me. I tell the woman, "This is the only time we can visit. We want to take a photo of the street we were found on." My stomach knots while speaking, "and the police station we were delivered to."

"Fine," the woman says, still gazing into the computer. After a minute, she sighs, then flips through a few papers from atop the desk. When she finds what she's looking for, she approaches us and drops the book on the table. It lands next to me with a bang.

"You need to sign that. We need your file number," she utters and returns to her desk.

Jenette and I exchange bewildered shrugs. I dig through my purse for a pen, not wanting to bother her any more than necessary. I enter my name, address, and file number, along with other information, onto its page. Jenette does the same. Then we wait at her mercy to be acknowledged again.

After a minute or so, without looking up from the computer screen, she states, "Your file is not here."

"What? What do you mean?"

"Your file is not here."

"Why?"

"Holt International moved years ago."

"I did not know that," I say, staring at my twin.

"Well, it's not here." She stands again, yawns, arches an aching back, and leaves the row of desks to approach us. "The international office is located in Oregon. That's where the files are. You need to go there."

Jenette and I reflect identical shrugs, again. I falter, "Oh, but I thought. We thought. Isn't this Holt International?"

Because my twin works full time, she left the researching and communicating with Holt to me. She did not have the time to search, and she also didn't really know the right questions to ask or even where to begin. I barely knew what to ask, and I had lots of time before the trip to contemplate and plan. We're speechless.

"Again," the woman states, "Holt International moved years ago."

I ignore her puffed-up attitude. "Hmm. The *Korea Post* didn't tell me this," I say. *Why didn't she send us a response e-mail about this change when we contacted her a few weeks ago? Why didn't she tell us to communicate with the Oregon Office for our records?*

"This is what happens," the woman says, towering over me to finish her comment, "when you have other people working for you."

Sitting as if a schoolgirl, I lean back in an attempt to escape her critical gaze. I also try to understand where she's coming from. *What the hell?* I sense the presence of years of frustration or even anger toward every adoptee who has ever stepped into the post-adoption services office looking for their birth records, asking stupid questions, wanting to know details about their lives, their history, and their identity. I'm just the next idiot in line. It takes a few seconds to collect my thoughts. "Are you. Are you lecturing me?"

"No," she sighs. "I'm just sick and tired of adoptees who think they have a right to barge in here and demand their birth file without an appointment. Some of them have even been caught trying to steal them," she discloses.

Stunned by the social worker's attitude, Jenette waits by the entrance, not wanting to be a disturbance, not knowing what our rights are; I study the "chick" our age, trying to comprehend the root cause beneath her hostile attitude.

"You should have contacted Holt in Oregon," she continues to tell us. "Not us."

I'm totally confused. Isn't this Holt Post Adoption Services? I reflect on my experience and past history. For thirty-two years, I've been the "good little girl," compliant to the rules, guidelines, and authority, not thinking about myself or my rights—not even thinking I *deserved* rights.

"Wait a minute," the social worker interrupts our silent shock. "I'll be right back," she says, and then she leaves the room. *Has she remembered something? Is there information in a drawer she's just remembered?*

Jenette plops on a chair next to me. Side by side, we gaze in space and wait.

A few minutes later, the woman is back with a new crème file folder. Opening it up, she shows me its contents: the latest letters of correspondence, the e-mail, and the faxes. "We only have the stuff you've just recently sent us," she says, sifting through the letters I had sent.

Jenette and I don't respond. We just stare and think, unable to absorb anything the woman flashes in front of us.

"And this." The social worker pulls out two stale-smelling wrinkled slips of paper from under the pile, dated back to the early nineteen seventies, documenting our milk intake in handwriting. But, strangely, that's it—no *real information leading us to the street.*

It takes a moment for my mind to process the papers. I feel like I'm taking up too much of the social worker's precious time. *If Holt International had moved all their files to Eugene, Oregon, why wouldn't they choose the entire folder and all of its contents? Why would both Jenette's and my milk intake form be kept in only one new folder? Since we have separate identification numbers, wouldn't we have our own files? Did she go in a back room, grab two meaningless papers and shove them into one file folder to serve as a pacifier? Doesn't she know that pacifiers only soothe one's thirst temporarily and artificially? Where's the rest of our information? What we need is the real deal.* I am suspicious but have no idea why. Why did I not trust them?

"See. We have nothing on you two," the social worker insists, shuffling through my file as if they are meaningless pieces of recyclable paper. "We only have your most recent faxes. All other documents are in Oregon. I have nothing here to give you. You should have contacted the Oregon office."

Mr. Lee, dressed in a suit and tie for what was supposed to be a celebratory occasion, lightly nudges me to pull out my book and show the young social worker, assuming it might sway her to be "impressed" as he had been and make an effort to help. Maybe she'll be sympathetic to our search and give us more information.

Much like letting the cat out of the bag, I reluctantly pull out my memoir *Twins Found in a Box: Adapting to Adoption.* "I wrote this book," I admit flatly, not wanting to use my status as an "author" to get more than I deserved.

The woman folds her arms over a disapproving chest and huffs. "You were not found in a box."

"What? I wasn't? We weren't? What do you mean? How do you know?" Trying to comprehend the information, I slip my book—as if an evil feline—back into the bag, embarrassed that the title of my memoir is really a lie. "That's what my parents always told me."

"No. There were no boxes." Her tone is cold. "Agencies placed drop boxes at police stations so mothers could easily leave their babies there for the employees to later pick up and gather at designated 'drop' boxes. But you were not literally found in a box." The woman acts as an authority on behalf of my history, sealed by the knowledge that only she and others in her position have access to.

There were no boxes? Weren't all Korean babies found abandoned in cardboard boxes along dirt and dusty streets in the 1970s? Wasn't it normal for hundreds of thousands of poor Korean parents to dump their babies? Wasn't this part of the Korean culture? Aren't Korean citizens emotionless people who place little to no importance on children—especially girls? No boxes? Only drop boxes provided by the adoption agencies? Doesn't make sense.

I stand to leave like a 'civilized' human being despite feeling totally inept. Jenette follows, and we linger by the exit, just staring at each other for a few moments, not knowing what to say aloud but reading each other's minds. *Is it normal for adoptees to take only what's been dished to us? Or are we asking for too much?* The young woman's comments continue to haunt me when we walk out of the office. *Why do adoptees feel the need to steal their birth files?*

Approaching the exit, two older adoptees arrive and wait at the counter, the same as we did, and for several minutes. Jenette and I watch to see if they received any answers. At first, the social worker does not acknowledge them. However, eventually, she asks the two what must be the standard question. "Do you have an appointment?"

The older one hesitantly whispers, "No," speaking for both of them.

It becomes apparent to me that I'm not the only one who has no idea what our rights to the family tree are.

On the way back to the hotel, the two men stare at Jenette and me with concerned eyes, waiting to see how we will react, unable to give support, intrigued at us because we're the first "American" females they've ever met. We remain still and quiet, trying to process this data. I'm embarrassed to have stolen their time for such unsuccessful results. Breaking the silence in the car, I softly say, "We came to Korea, not expecting anything. If we're supposed to find our parents, we will." The car ride back to the hotel is silent thereafter.

What have other adoptees done? Would we recognize our parents if they passed by? According to a Korean friend in the states, she suspects our birth parents could be on Jeju-Do Island. She says that because we have darker than usual Korean skin, we could be islanders. And it's the last spot on the travel itinerary. So, during our visit to Jeju-Do, I'll keep my eyes open for anyone who resembles us. For now, Jenette and I feel lucky. We have each other, at least! Siblings, we've overheard, have even been sent to separate homes—even different nations! We've been fortunate to have been brought up together.

Lifestyles of the Rich and Famous

*Though I am grateful for the blessings of wealth,
it hasn't changed who I am. My feet are still on the ground.
I'm just wearing better shoes.*
—Oprah Winfrey, O Magazine

When Jenette and I return to the Sofitel, the conference ceremonies have formally begun. White double doors are opened, revealing a grand ballroom where numerous adoptees sent around the world have congregated, inducing introductions and forging friendships, at last. Name tags show where we are from and when we had been adopted. Enormous chandeliers hang from two-story ceilings resembling glistening spider webs beset with frozen dew. On a front stage, flags representing fifteen countries stand at ease on brass posts. Spotlights shine on a large banner above the flags announcing, "Welcome, Adoptees, to Seoul, Korea!" The official logo for the Gathering and those of thirteen participating contributors complement the sign. Giant white and gray panels in a traditional English décor border the gym-sized space, and the place looks elegant. It is evident that the organizers made every effort to make the event memorable.

The staff and the participants meander around the display tables, exploring the grand ballroom. The Koreans around me have eyes as sweet as dark chocolate and smiles that energize the hotel lobby and halls. The staff bow at Jenette and me when we walk by. *Intriguing. This is definitely not my hometown.*

Gifts from individuals and organizations cover large tables. We attack them the same way we did the all-you-can-eat buffet. A full-colored program book serves as a backbone to the conference, giving us an itinerary, a brief historical overview of the Korean Adoptee Community, and a photo directory of the attending adoptees. On the first twenty pages, goodwill messages from the organizers, government officials, non-profit organizations, ministers, representatives, and international Korean adoptee associations welcome us. The program's professionalism and high-quality design affirm the importance of the event. Other gifts include books from several organizations: The Artists Program Book showcasing the work of adoptee artists, created specifically for the Gathering; an Overseas Korean Artist Yearbook (O.K.A.Y.); and a book called *Love, Life, and Light: The Story of Mother of Asia* by Chung Soo Park. We're also given many guidebooks, brochures, and maps, helping to shed light on our missed culture. I'm so glad to be a member of this group of lovely people!

More than four hundred Korean adoptees chat and mingle, filling the hotel with Western-style and perspectives. Travelers reunite with old friends; others find new ones. I snap a few photos of the crowd, intoxicated by the presence of so many adoptees. The European accents and dress intrigue me, and we can point them out. They have an artistic and alternative type of style that is hard to explain but easy to establish. The men and women wear their hair in a longer shag-type style, compared to those of us who were sent to the U.S., who sport either military cuts for the men or straight perms on the women. The European females dress in artsy styles; American women wear slacks, blouses, and suit jackets. Living such a sheltered life separated from other adoptees, my curiosity increases. *What were their lives like? Anything like mine? Are they happy with their fate? Was there pain? Was it joyful? Have they, yet, encountered a reunion? Do they even want to?*

Jenette and I miss the opening ceremony's welcoming remarks, and instead, we are interviewed by media with the hope that we look familiar to someone out there. We don't have much time. According to the conference schedule, we have until Sunday before we leave for the after-conference tour, which will take us away from the city and to the country's outer edge. Activities run from early morning into the night. We want to try to attend to everything.

The prospect of finding our parents via the media brings hope and tension. Photographers and reporters from around the world prowl the lobby, attempting to slide into the events and private discussion groups even though everything is planned exclusively for adoptees. Ready to write stories, they ask Jenette and me if we know the whereabouts of certain individuals. We're unable to recognize each Korean name until they ask for *Kim, Myung Ja,* and *Kim, Moon Ja.* Wait a minute. I think for a moment. These names sound so familiar. *Duh! That's my name! That's Jenette's name! They've asked for our Korean names! Oh my gosh. That's us!* They've been asking for adoptees by Korean names, but few adoptees respond to their Korean names. My Korean name is just a word on a piece of paper, presumably given to me by the adoption agency. It sounds as foreign as other Korean names.

When I say, "Hey, that's me. Myung Ja Kim is me," and yank out the photo identification necklace identifying Jenette and me, the journalists ask to interview us.

"What do you want to do if you find your birth mother?" They inquire before we find a couch to sit on.

"Shopping," I say, followed by a smile, not knowing what else to add. What else does a daughter do with a mother? Growing up in the states, we didn't spend "quality" time with our adoptive mother, but it didn't bother me. I assumed we were a pretty average middle-class American family. I remember waiting with Dad and my brothers in the white Limousine while Mom went into JC Penney or Sears to exchange or return an outfit after church on Sundays. I don't remember actually going into the store with her and loitering around the make-up counters or the clothes racks. "Shopping" is the only answer I can think of, and so that's what I divulge to curious media people. Mom had used to clothes shop for Jenette and me before school started, but we didn't go inside the mall with her. "Shopping," I say, as if hanging out at the mall is fun for me.

By this time, we slip into a sitting area surrounded by photographers, television crews, and journalists. Old photos of our life in America are strewn on the coffee table, and suddenly a life with the Swans seems idyllic—the answer to every problem.

Korean men and women, with press tags, are awed at the old images of our childhood. Mom has the six of us dressed in expensive, thick, faux fur coats. My parent's smile eradicates any evidence of melancholy. The photos don't paint the entire picture.

Mom spent weekdays on the living room couch, not socializing with anyone, not even the neighbors. I wished she'd gotten more involved. I spent my childhood praying she might do something with her life besides watching television and making secretive shopping trips that temporarily satiated her shopaholic cravings and binges. I do not consider my childhood as bad. I know Mom tried the best she could to raise her children the "right-winged" way. Life with the swans was pretty average—pretty ordinary. We have no complaints.

I remember living under a collage of Pacific Northwest conifers, where tall pines, junipers, Douglas firs, hemlocks, spruce, and grand firs greeted us daily, waving dark tree branches. Mom and Dad were proud because they were the first to choose a lot when the city wasn't a city, and the land was a vast forest with barely used roads. I remember falling asleep and waking up to tree branches swaying nearby. The view stretched as far as we could see. I remember pine, fir, and hemlock cones dropping all around, long pine needles like whisk brooms, spruce needles that pricked fingers, droopy juniper branches that beckoned at us with long arms, and the odor of green conifers now available as car fresheners for a dollar ninety-nine. But, as much as I loved Mom, I don't remember what color her eyes were.

I remember the shiny leaves of English holly, the constant itch from stinging nettles, eating huckleberries, and pruning the ferns scattered throughout our acre-plus yard. I remember trying to drown slugs—especially the disgusting pea-green ones. I remember collecting and trying to figure out how to kill termites in a tin cup and trying to help garter snakes shed their skin—believing I was doing them a favor. I remember trying to find the frogs in the creek down the backyard bank and studying the cute little dead moles the cats brought to the front door for us. Built beneath such a masculine spread of conifers and maple trees, the sun could barely reach us at the house. I liked the land I grew up in, but it was cold.

I'm pulled out of my recall with multiple microphones waving in front of us. We're asked: "Why do you want to find your birth mother?"

"So we can go shopping," I repeat to whoever is listening with pen and paper, having no idea what I really wanted to do. Truthfully, when the honeymoon stage is over, and all is said and done, it might be cool to discuss a variety of topics, such as our favorites that have to do with philosophy, religion, literature, mythology, psychology, or spirituality. Mostly I just want the truth.

Even without that "perfect" mother, whether adoptive or biological, I am at peace and happy. I believe I've had a fulfilling life and do not feel that my past would have been better or worse with my biological parents. I just can't help, at this moment, to wonder. Who knows, tomorrow I might not care.

"May we take a few photos of you two," a journalist says. "Scoot together."

Jenette and I comply. The first interviewer tells us the paper he writes for is equivalent to the *LA Times*; another reporter boasts his paper is the largest in Seoul.

"Lean into each other."

"Okay," we chime, then tilt our heads, wondering who will read the articles written concerning us or how far into the country the newspapers will reach and hoping someone will point us out.

"Now hold hands," we're told.

Jenette and I look at each other, noses scrunched. "Gross! No way," we exclaim.

"What? Why?" the interviewer asks, perplexed. "Why won't you hold hands?"

"No," Jenette says.

I explain, "We've never been a close family."

"We've never held hands," my twin adds. "We don't hug or hold hands in America."

The crew studies us. We must be the oddest ducks they've ever met. "But, Americans have the reputation of being much more affectionate," they tell us.

Jenette and I face each other and laugh. "That's just a stereotype. Not our family. We were never affectionately open," I say. Even sitting next to each other is too close for comfort. Our family rarely gave hugs.

After a back-and-forth exchange, they concede, letting us sit together, heads tilted together but hands separated.

"What is it like to grow up in the states?" we're asked, and "How wonderful is it in America?"

I don't know quite which way to turn or how to answer. I remember this past summer: I paid for our kids' swimming lessons, but the manager at the counter "forgot" to give us the free passes to use the pool like she was supposed to. I think about how the manager had crossed her arms when I stopped my vehicle in the parking lot, blocking me from entering the pool building, and how she asked in a condescending tone (assuming I didn't understand English) if she could help me. I intuited her subtext: *could she help me leave the premises.* My gut told me she couldn't *see* me; she merely saw my physicality—as if I was an illegal alien who wanted to steal jobs—instead of seeing me as a human who could potentially be her friend and assist. I think about the way I've been trained to ignore subtle discrimination as if it doesn't exist.

I reflect on my childhood so long ago; any racial incidents barely matter. Even if I had been faced with blunt racism, I'd still be a loyal fan of the nation I was raised in. As a minority, you must, or there's more reason for the massive population to hate you. I am excited about the future. Fortunately, the United States is improving so that each individual, regardless of location and ethnicity, is discovering (one way or another) we humans are more the same than different; we all hold the same hope for peace and harmony. I still detect disapproval against my race in mostly rural areas and suburbs, but an awakening is on the horizon. Hence, do I give the Korean Press the answer they expect to hear?

I smile at the newspaper reporters and sweetly say what everyone expects to hear: "America is amazing!"

Unforgotten Sons

*Knowing yourself goes far deeper
than the adoption of a set of ideas or beliefs.
—Eckhart Tolle,
A New Earth: Awakening to Your Life's Purpose*

The conference begins the following morning as registration continues. Korean children, sent to Australia, Belgium, Canada, Denmark, France, Germany, Luxemburg, Netherlands, Norway, Sweden, Switzerland, UK, and, of course, many from the U.S., are now Western adults, and we line up in the upstairs lobby to sign-in. We're an unusual culture—the only culture whose members have grown and been raised separately, detached from their origin, resembling each other merely by ethnicity and circumstance. Every other society has a history of unification, filled with rituals, rites, and rights to the original family, and when they migrate, they migrate together—always together. Ethnicity seems to affirm that there is something bigger than who a person is— something recognizably significant an individual actually belongs to. Without a group to totally identify with, it's not uncommon to feel "wrong" and isolated at times. Something inside tells me that we, adoptees, don't let our lot in life get us down. We are so good at thriving—*and on our own!*

Many adult adoptee groups have taken time and money to put together this grand event, opening doors to Seoul for those adoptees who might not have made a trip without the benefit of supportive members. Opportunities to mingle range from Korean art and cultural activities to workshops and panel discussions. Jenette and I cannot attend every event, as many overlap. Our top priority, if we can't find our birth parents, is to have fun with other adoptees.

Breakfast is set up buffet style in the grand ballroom. Options range from everything offered in the United States, plus unfamiliar fruits, biscuits, and yogurts offered in South Korea. Even in the morning, the formality of the large ballroom resembles that of a glamorous black-tie event, albeit most of us sport professional clothes—as suggested. After eating, adoptees divide into groups according to age to partake in the workshops spread throughout different areas of the hotel.

In Jenette and my age group, there are probably 75 participants. The vast majority of the adoptees are successful, at least it appears so. There are many happily-ever-after fairy tales to be told. I'm impressed with everyone. *Wow.* Together, at last, we're a great group of people, greater than I could ever imagine. For once in our lives, Jenette and I wholeheartedly fit into a large group! Adoptees can be found in every professional arena: entertainment, the medical field, politics, education, and sports.

Only adoptees are allowed inside these discussion groups. This is a rare opportunity—perhaps even a once-in-a-lifetime opportunity—for us to squawk and squeal on being the "adopted" one without being judged, questioned, or argued with. In these sessions, we give personal accounts using our "insider's" perspective rather than that promoted by adoption agencies, community, and adoptive parents—each presumes to know better for us and can't quite imagine our outlook within the adoptive nest, neighborhood, and nation. Even inside blue skies, there are limits!

For the first time, I'm learning at each workshop that the adoptee experience has not been 100 percent heavenly. In fact, everyone here is pretty open with various feelings. It's easy to overflow with emotion, emotions I've, in the past, hardly paid attention to. Have I been going around a blind and blissful birdie? I feel as if I've been living in La La Land (maybe a little flighty), as if I've followed the utopian fantasy of how life *should* be rather than facing the ground as it is. I'm surprised that these adoptees' perspectives have not been taken seriously, within or even outside of the industry.

According to a published survey from Evan B. Donaldson at the 1999 Gathering held in Washington D.C., seventy percent of the Korean-born adoptees cited that they had been discriminated against while growing up in the communities they were sent to. Many had been picked on with bigoted remarks *inside* the home they were sent to. Seventy-one percent grew up in small towns or rural areas. Seventy percent grew up in Caucasian neighborhoods.[4]

Are adoption agencies sending children to loving, welcoming societies? Outside of conference activities, I overhear one "unknown" adoptee ask, "Better societies for whom? A better society, to me, is not a racist society." Another "unknown" adoptee pointed out how, as she grew into an adult, she realized that she could no longer think of herself as a Caucasian person. Sadly, she grew to understand that society has not and will not be able to perceive her as a true American or a real Korean. Both societies judge her in one way or another. How has this attitude affected internationally adopted children? And how does this attitude affect us as we grow into adults?

I'm also learning that parenthood sparks the curiosity for one's blood ties for most adoptees. I think this is most evident for those who do not have Korean siblings. About two-thirds of the group have, at one time, tried to find relatives. The birth of my children did not elicit the need to search for my Korean family—maybe because I've always had my twin around. One-third of the group has no desire or is ambivalent towards making a re-connection, reflecting my attitude before the trip. I think another deterrent preventing adoptees from searching is the risk of hurting or deceiving our adoptive parents. Why jeopardize their affection? Our search for our Korean family could be construed as unfaithfulness and disrespectfulness, making everyone's lives more complicated. Juggling more parents might cause uneasiness between the two sets of folks we're tied to.

I've learned that it is normal for a change in identity to occur at some point in our lives. Adoption professionals and so-called experts have labeled this change an "identity crisis," but I think of it as more of an identity *revelation*. As children, we identify ourselves as "Caucasian" on applications and such that ask for our race. Then as adults, we identify ourselves as "Asian." We're born with certain feathers but tethered to others. Then during adulthood, we can't help but acknowledge that we're not the same swans we've been told we were. Life as an "unknown" bird is cuckoo. *Cuckoo!*

The hotel café is identical to a Seattle coffee shop. Soft incandescent lights and table lamps illuminate each sitting area. Adoptees are scattered throughout the place. The sound of milk being frothed, the pounding of coffee grounds, and the whirl of blenders can be heard reminiscent of a choir of café vibrations above people's rumbling voices. Adoptees gather round in groups of threes and fours, their hands moving animatedly while talking. Laughter and excited voices flood the café. I can see that, like Jenette and me, everyone is glad to be here.

Once I order my own cup of coffee, I wait for Jenette to meet me at a table next to another group. She must be hanging out with Christina or had found more twins. While I slowly sip from a white ceramic mug, the voices from behind seduce me to eavesdrop while I wait. A woman mentions an adoption agency, and the topic stirs my interest. Somewhat muffled, I hear her divulge rumors to her partner. "Did you know an American couple is suing New Beginnings agency?"

"What?" Another voice says, "What are you talking about?"

"Yes. I heard that their case has something to do with agency lies."

"Lies? Lies about what?"

"Something that has to do with unethical practices. When the couple first adopted, the agency told them that the seven-year-old boy they had available came from a woman who was unmarried and that she was too poor to raise him. The agency also claimed that he had no other family."

"Sounds pretty typical. Many of the Korean mothers were too poor to take care of their children back in the old days."

"But this was as recently as 1989. It's a current case. The adopting couple found out the agency lied about their son's origin. The truth was that the boy's jealous stepmother dropped the boy off at the orphanage, giving him a different last name while doing so. But the father and the rest of his family still loved and wanted him."

"Well, did the father even look for his son?" The other woman seems skeptical.

"Yes, he did. In fact, as soon as two days later, he arrived at the orphanage asking for him, but the staff refused to release his son because of the name change. The father didn't know his girlfriend used a different name when she gave him to the agency. So the father ended up registering him as lost on the national rolls, never realizing that the boy's name had been changed."

"Sounds like a big misunderstanding to me."

"Once the adoptee learned how to speak English, he finally did complain to his adoptive parents. But by then, he was already a teen, and he was their son for ten years."

"Could be typical teenage rebellion," the other voice surmised.

At this time, I turn around and grab a magazine from a nearby coffee table, hoping to sneak a peek at the two women. I fully expect to see Caucasians based on their English. Nope. They're Korean. The second woman's hair is cut short against the nape of her neck, and she appears to be much older than me. I can't see the face of the first woman, but based on the tone of her voice, she might be older than me. The women continue their conversation, unaware that I'm eavesdropping.

"Actually, the boy said he hated the photo ID tag the agency had taken of him from the beginning. He stated that they took away his real name and when they photographed him, they even took away the denim jacket his father gave him *and* his father's business card—the only thing he had that identified his father."

"That's hard to believe."

"It's true. I read it in a New York Metro newspaper."

"Hmm. I still can't believe it."

"But listen to this! When the adoptive parents contacted the agency a second time, for the truth, they were told the second lie."

"What? That can't be true."

"The agency alleged that the boy had been badly neglected while his mother was at work and that he roamed the streets to fend for himself, which warranted his need to be sent to a better family."

"But isn't that pretty typical in Korea? Don't *all* Korean parents leave their children to fend for themselves? That's what I've always believed."

"I don't know. Could be. At least that's the picture the agencies paint. But when the adoptive parents told the agency of the boy's memories of his father, the agency claimed the boy's memories were 'pure fantasy.'"

There's a silence between the two women, and I can't help but scrutinize what I've just heard. It seems unbelievable. Incomprehensible. But then I think if the employees at the adoption agency could lie twice, I ponder a strange concept: How many times have they lied before and to how many people? Something doesn't feel right.

"Well," the dubious woman asks, "what made the adoptive parents decide to actually sue the agency?"

"From what I gathered," the informant says, "the article said that when the adoptee reached his teenage years, he became depressed with a bit of anger. He even screamed at them, 'You are not my parents! You wanted a son, and the people were willing to sell me, and you bought me!'"[5]

"How rude to his adoptive parents. Sounds like an ungrateful teenager to me."

"Yes. But the adoptive parents are on their son's side."

"They are?" The older woman asks.

"Yes. His mother said that forcing the boy to assume a false identity had taken them to 'hell and back,' so now they're charging the agency with negligence, breach of contract, and fraud, making for one of the largest lawsuits against an agency by adoptive parents."[8]

For fifteen minutes, I listen carefully, wondering if fraud has been a prevalent practice. Could my sister and I be victims of agency lies, and this is the reason behind the hesitance to give answers? Shocking! For our entire lives, we've been told we were orphans found in a box! We've always been told we had been abandoned! What if we weren't? What if we came from a real family, secretly tricked? I gotta tell Jenette. Where is she? Why is she late?

One Nation Under God

To believe with certainty, we must begin with doubting.
—Stanislaw Leszczynski

I leave my seat with coffee in hand to stand by the lounge entrance and wait for my sister. Every three minutes, I glance at the clock across the lobby set at military time. She's late. I watch adoptees loiter and overhear chit-chat on awestruck reunions with Korean families. Between conference workshops and sessions, Jenette and I had planned to meet at this particular café. After twenty minutes of tapping my foot, sighing, and growing impatient, I notice my sister spill out of the second elevator on the right side and dash my way. She's bursting with energy. Her purse flies into the air when she bumps into me, almost knocking off my black-rimmed glasses.

"Oh, my God! Did you meet the French twins?"

"No. Why?" I ask, perturbed, pushing my glasses back into place.

"They are s-o-o cute! These guys are from France."

"That figures," I say sarcastically.

"And they can speak English too!"

"Cool," I say without heart. I'm too focused on the rumors. Jenette must know something is up, but she continues to push me into a good mood.

"One has glasses. One doesn't." She smirks because I've been wearing my glasses during this trip, and she hasn't.

"Nice."

"One of them is in journalism, and the other one works for a T.V. Station."

"Cool."

"But I can't tell them apart yet. This is going to be hard. I hope I don't get them confused. That would be s-o-o embarrassing!" She pants, out of breath. Noticing I'm *not* as excited as she is, she asks, "What's wrong?"

I grab her arm and lead her into the cafe. On the way to the table and then settling down, I whisper a quick version of the latest gossip. Adoptees speak well when referring to their adoptive families. We assume adoptive parents have done the best they could. Life in Asia, we've been told by them, would have been "horrible." If we hadn't been sent to the West, we might have been given only a handful of rice as a daily ration. We would have been beggars and prostitutes. That's the prevailing theory and the narrative the adoption industry is founded upon.

Today, we have lots to be thankful for. Thoughts of ever living or visiting Korea had rarely ever entered our minds, so being here seems pretty surreal. Before arriving, I had assumed my motherland was dirt poor, nothing special, even Godless. But for an unknown reason, I'm in tune with surfacing rumors about the "hidden side" of adoption, possibly due to agencies' sins.

After bringing up the topic about the Korean boy whose adoptive parents are currently suing the agency, Jenette is just as surprised as I am: "What?" she asks, settling down. "You mean he wasn't an orphan in the first place?"

"Nope."

"No way."

We attempt to soak in the thought. We've been told we were found on a street corner. What if the line was a lie? "I can barely believe it myself," I admit.

"But that's a big deal!" My sister conceals her astonishment in a whisper. "Orphan status is the whole reason we were said to be adopted."

"I also heard how social workers have been called bloodsuckers due to high demand from the West. By the time the 1988 Olympics rolled around, adoption agencies were getting away with sending around 8,000 Korean babies to the West each year."[6]

"Oh, my God." She spills coffee onto a white ceramic saucer. "But, Korea is such a small country. I mean, it's a tiny nation, about the size of Washington State."

"In another newspaper report, a former social worker said she was assigned to seven hospitals and clinics. She was supposed to cultivate the babies. She'd go to the hospital and talk to the mothers. Ask them to sign papers."[7]

"Wow."

"During the Olympics, the Koreans came under scrutiny for selling their babies because the war had ended thirty-some years ago. The public wondered why Korea still sent their children overseas. In a 1988 article called 'Babies for Sale. South Koreans Make Them, Americans Buy Them,' it was written that, at first, the Korean mothers didn't want to give up their babies. Most of them weren't even in poverty, and the majority of us aren't orphans."[8]

"No way." My sister's eyes bulge at this disclosure. "I don't understand. Most of us weren't even orphans in the first place?"

I nod. "According to what I hear, the director of an agency said ninety percent of mothers wanted to keep their babies, but after counseling, only around ten percent kept them. Social workers suggested that it wasn't a good idea to keep the baby without the biological father."[9]

"No way. That's totally inconsiderate toward the mother!" My sister exclaims. As a single mother, she knows.

"I know," I say, agreeing. "And the father. ...If they thought the parents were too young or didn't have enough money, social workers would suggest the couple give the baby away. No one ever saw anything wrong with this."

"That's ludicrous. That reminds me of when Mom wanted me to give Dustin up for adoption. Thank God I didn't listen to her! Dustin is my life. He's a huge reason why I live."

I nod, remembering a time that seemed so long ago. We were young and rebellious, thank God. I'm so glad Jenette didn't submit to Mom's rules. Recalling how afraid I was during my own two pregnancies causes me to become angry at the thought. Yes, I was married, and my husband and I lived in a comfortable apartment, but both of us were still nervous about whether or not we'd make good parents. I would have hated it if someone tried to talk us out of our daughters, based on who we were then.

"They shouldn't even put the thought into a mother's head!" I criticize my surfacing emotions. Not wanting to make a scene, I lower my voice. "Especially at the time of a woman's pregnancy. Everyone is crazy when they're pregnant. Even wealthy American women who are in their thirties and forties and have everything they could possibly want to have doubts regarding their parenting abilities."

"I know! I have yet to meet anyone totally confident and prepared. Does that mean our Korean parents could have been counseled out of keeping us?" My sister asks.

"Could be. It's been reported recently that most Korean kids come into the adoption program through Holt's Unwed Mothers Program in Korea. Out of 1,120 births at sixteen centers that supposedly provide what the agency calls "Protection Services," only fifteen percent kept their babies. For example, in one year, seventy-three percent or 824 babies were sent abroad."[10]

"That's ridiculous," Jenette protests, now engrossed. "How could agencies do that?"

"They think they're doing God a big favor. Did you notice in Holt's 2002 *Love in Action* booklet, it reported that less than ten Korean children, out of 1,520, had been sent overseas due to the possibility of missing or deceased parents? The rest came from families."

"Unbelievable." Jenette sighs and plops against the back of the chair. A minute passes, and we're both still stuck in thought. I feel a bit guilty for tainting the trip for her with shocking news, but then I think that I'm only the messenger. I can barely believe the news myself.

To think that our Korean mother could have been given religious counseling or told that Westerners make better, more loving parents seems to me to be a violation of her rights—the rights Mother Nature and Father Time gave her. Why didn't the agencies provide encouragement and support? I answer my own question. Duh. It didn't pay. My intuition suggests that something big is going on; I can sense grief rising in my diaphragm.

I stare through the large window, barely seeing the buses, cabs, and limousines. At the moment, Seoul envelops us in the vein of a sanctuary even though it's a large active city. I did not expect this before the trip. Over ten million people live within city limits, placing Seoul sixth on the list of the most heavily populated in the world. In comparison, New York City ranks tenth with about eight million residents.[11]

My twin glances at her watch and gathers her bags, then stands. "I gotta go." Her fluster of activity breaks me out of my thoughtful spell.

"Wait. Don't you want to know more?"

"I've got plans. I've made promises."

"Wait—" I urge, rushing to gather up my own books and pamphlets.

"No. Seriously. I gotta go." She says.

"Why?"

"I gotta meet up with the French twins. I wanna see if I can tell them apart." My twin blazes around the corner and is gone in a flash. I saunter out of the café alone, hoping that I'm just obsessed over made-up fears that actually have nothing to do with reality. In fact, I feel guilty for even suspecting that anyone separates uninformed and inexperienced parents from their offspring—their own flesh and blood—for money. How dare I question the agency's integrity! Most likely, the industry is not as bad as my intuition suggests. Knowing that my imagination can get out of hand with worst-case scenarios, I decided to e-mail my children and husband and let them know that everything is okay. I wouldn't want them to think I've been kidnapped over here!

Mystery Man

If you don't risk anything, you risk even more.
—Erica Jong

Between conference activities, I search for a computer that will give me a connection to the World Wide Web so I can send e-mails. Sometimes, I use the business office late at night when everyone is asleep. Then I heard of an Internet café outback and underground. I check it out and find it convenient. Stuffed in a basement with at least twenty computers, the fluorescent lighting and small fans of the room can't dispel the clammy cave heat. But the prices to get online are at only 10,000 won per hour—maybe a dollar compared to at least five times that amount inside the air-conditioned hotel. I keep my family updated, letting them know we've arrived and we're fine, even though the post-adoption agency refused to give us complete records. I won't let the agency ruin our celebrations in Seoul.

Practically out of breath, I'm marching back up the alley after sending my e-mails when I notice a Korean man ahead looking down the hill at me. It looks as if he's been sitting in a shiny black car, and as soon as I exited the Internet café, he steps out of the vehicle. *What the heck?* He doesn't look away. He just keeps staring at me. *Why? Is he waiting for a loved one?* I turn around to see if he's looking for someone behind me. *Nope, just a parking garage swallowing a crooked cement road,* and it appears as if few cars come down this way. The hotel stands on my left, and a tiny mart and aging housing sit on my right. This puts me on guard. I've been told that South Korea is a dangerous place. I'm used to always being aware of my surroundings. We tourists are supposed to watch out for ourselves at all times whenever traveling to any country outside the U.S. Don't want to be trapped in Seoul!

But, as much as I hate to admit it and as much as I avoid the news, bad things can happen in the U.S., as well. In the U.S., women and children have been raped, murdered in parks, cities, and even inside their own homes. When I was a teen, a man jerked to a stop along the curb beside me, opened his car door, and urged me to get in as if he thought I was a prostitute while I walked home from my job at an ice cream shop. I stalled, stared, then slammed his car door shut. He got angry but luckily sped off. It was a close call. Those were the days of the "Green River Murderer," a man later convicted of murdering around 50 or so women from the 1960s to 1989. It was written that the murderer had pulled up past one of his victims and opened the front passenger door to get her inside. Dead women had been found near the college my sister attended.

I was raised to constantly be cautious and wary of strangers. The "pretty perfect" suburb we grew up in could be a dangerous place—same as any place in the U.S. Always stand at least an arm's length away. Keep valuables tightly hidden inside our clothing. Don't wear long strap purses that can be used to choke. Jab at the neck or eyes if problems occur. Try to memorize the attacker's appearance. Never let them take you to the dreaded second location, even if a gun is shown. Better to be shot in public than in the woods. Always carry pepper spray or a small weapon, such as a knife. If all else fails, scream. The worst that can happen is to be kidnapped and snatched away from family.

This man keeps staring at me! What if he attacks? How will I go to the police or report misdemeanors if I don't even speak the language? I look for possible places to run just in case he decides to commit some sort of crime. There's a little mini grocery mart behind me, or I could go back down to the basement, or I could . . . . The hot, humid outside air is like being stuck inside a sauna. I'm so used to cool Seattle rain. Out of the hotel for only a short time, and already my body feels like sticky rice. Should I run, my cotton-polyester slacks and long sleeve top will feel like a wet blanket, slowing me down.

Approaching the Korean man, I mull over the idea of crossing the alley to avoid bumping into him, but when I look for oncoming traffic, he waves at me to "come here." Not the way Americans do it, with palm up. Waving with a palm up in Korea is only used to signal at dogs. He waves at me with a palm down, which ends up looking to an American as "go on" or "go away."

He's not intimidating-looking. He appears as if a typical Korean—not that I've talked with many. He's thin, dressed in slacks and a polo top; his thick black hair is touched with white resembling a gentle snowfall. A few strands in the back are pressed upward, just like my husband's does in the mornings. How endearing! My gut tells me he's not dangerous. Ever since I stepped foot in South Korea, I feel this unfamiliar sense of safety—as if acceptable for just being me, as there's nothing to prove, and despite my brown skin, "I'm tolerable." As a minority in the states, my every action is perceived as a representation of the entire Asian race and typically seen as *bad*. I'm an enemy or inferior to much of the population in the states, whether I like it or not. After a while, being judged by my Korean ethnicity can cause resentment to surface if I'm not careful.

It's because of my gut feeling that I choose to go ahead and approach the man—or maybe it's because I've been married to a "real" Asian man and rely on past experience. Despite the prevalent misunderstandings and assumptions made against men from the east, I've managed to deconstruct the sweeping generalizations and see Asians for who they truly are—some of the most considerate and modest people I have come across.

As I draw nearer to the Korean man, I notice fine lines and grief around his eyes. He looks to be around the age of forty to fifty. Most importantly, I sense the energy around him as harmless. Slightly shorter than my five-foot-eight husband, he doesn't appear dangerous. In fact, he exudes concern—not anger or manipulation. When I'm an arm's length away, he begins to ramble and won't stop. I feel a little fraudulent when I listen to him without saying a word in response. Judging by my ethnicity, he probably assumes I can understand him, and I either look completely rude and standoffish to him or entirely deaf and dumb. Sadly, I have no idea what he's fishing for, and I can't even tell him my inadequacies in what is supposed to be "my" language. I can only think for myself and hope he's not offended. *Is he lost? Why is he showing me a small blank book? Is he looking for a location? Is it a journal? Oh, it's an address book.* He pushes the pen towards my direction and then the book and taps the blank page. He speaks Korean then places the pen in my right hand. Suddenly, I wish I could speak "my" language. He wipes his brows with a cloth and sticks it into his pocket. Finally, a light bulb moment. *Duh! I am so retarded.* He wants me to write down my contact information. *I'm a total idiot in my motherland!* Against my wary upbringing, I scribble into the book my e-mail address. It seems to appease him. "Gam sa hamnida" is the only phrase he says that I understand. I think it means "thank you."

Taking a few steps to the side to leave, I nod at the man as if I understand his reasoning, but I don't. I have no idea what he wants. As soon as I turn around to leave, he touches my shoulder, apparently not yet finished. When he slips a hand into his front slack pocket, I think, *oh god, what have I gotten myself into?* But then he tugs out a white envelope and places it gently into both my hands. I exhale a sigh of relief. Still afraid to look at it, I notice right away that it's sealed and lumpy as if something thick is inside. A Western name is carefully written on top in light juvenile handwriting. I don't recognize her name but take the envelope anyway. Upon leaving, I'm unsure about accepting the note, and I can feel his eyes watching me enter the back door to the grand hotel. I shove the envelope into my pocket like a candy bar wrapper, wanting to open the thing and peek. But what if it's some sort of bomb threat? Part of me feels the urge to drop the note into the next garbage can and forget the strange man. *What if, by fulfilling this task, I'm contributing to a crime?* I know that my adoptive mother would have instructed me to be especially cautious. She was born in 1929, and foreign men were still not to be trusted even into the late 1980s—like when I first met the man I would later marry. This prevalent attitude hadn't changed much for some in the states even today—in 2004.

My gut tells me it's none of my business and that I should just find the named person and give the envelope to her as soon as I see her. I decide to keep it and wait until the opportunity to fulfill the Korean man's task while feeling uncertain. Every time I pass a garbage can, nerves nudge me to throw the envelope in. On the other hand, my curiosity has always been much stronger. In fact, my curiosity earned me the Asian man I chose to marry.

While I was growing up, there was never any mention of even one good Asian in the states—let alone an Asian man. In fact, everything about Korea was supposedly *bad*. Rare were those who could discern between the varying Asian ethnicities. I remember the day in 1988 when I first met my current husband. Due to his immigrant status, my adoptive mother immediately disapproved. I figured the automatic rejection had something to do with his race—but his race was mine, so any insult against him felt like an insult against me. Here at the conference, I couldn't help but notice that I was the only adoptee married to a full-blooded Asian man, making me feel like an anomaly. I found one other female adoptee married to an Asian, but both were adoptees and so acceptable according to the assumptions made by the adoption industry. I was definitely a rebellious malfunction in this community, but at the same time, I was proud. Our independence and rebelliousness rooted my husband and me to survive and then thrive.

Unforgotten Daughters

*You can take a person out of Asia.
But you can't take the Asian out of the person.
— A popular saying on Asian American television*

I'm waiting for Jenette and Christina at one of the elevators. We're supposed to meet here before getting on the bus for dinner and show at the Kwanmunsa Temple. At the elevators, I'm spacing out, still focused on wanting to know why the Korean man approached me. And who did the name on the envelope belong to?

"Scuse me. Yew lawst in thawt?" A young Korean stranger approaches togged up in (of all things) a black cowboy hat, and I'm not sure if he's talking to me or someone from behind. I turn around and find no one looking his way.

"Yew lawst in thawt?" The man asks again with a sharp Southern twang. His supersize grin tells me he knows my sister, and he thinks I'm her. It takes me a while to grasp his question, eventually realizing he's asking if 'I'm lost in thought.'

Pointing a finger against my chest, I ask, "Me?"

"Ah reckonize yew," he says, still showing off a mighty smile.

Unable to identify the man, I stumble over my words. "Umm. Uh. You probably know my twin sister."

"Yore Ja Nat, right?" He flashes me a nod of recognition.

"Actually, no. I'm her twin. I'm Janine."

The man removes his hat and hides it gently under the other arm, then extends a hand for me to shake. "My name's Pawl."

He grasps my hand with both of his. "Yore sister's mighty fahn. Ah met her yesterdee. Ya all luke the same!"

It's so unusual to hear this Korean man stand in front of me and speak with a Southern accent that I'm not sure if I'm seeing or hearing him right. I'm sure his twang sounds stronger than it really is because of our location here in Seoul. It takes me a moment to digest his words and realize he's saying that my sister is fine. I smile at his comment. Everyone who passes me seems to think that I'm her or they know me because of her. By now, I'm used to the mistaken identity. It used to happen a lot during our school years.

"Ah herd ya'll had trouble at the agency."

"Yeah. The social worker refused to give us our history. Or any information to help us find our birth parents."

"Same here. Ah found out while back, Ah had a brother. Both of us were sent to the U.S."

"Oh, my gosh. Are you guys twins?"

"Nah. We're only a yer apart. We're bounden determined to git to knowin' each otha cause we're kin. Ah plan to fly on over and meet 'em after the gatherin."

"Wow. It must be so strange to meet a sibling for the first time as an adult."

"Ah've been lookin' fer my berth family since I turned eighteen. We've been real lucky. We both speak American. Ah was sent to the South, and my brother was sent to the North," he tells me.

Barely able to understand him, I agree, "Yeah. At least you'll be able to communicate." Geez. I suddenly think I'm fortunate to be adopted with my sis. What if I had found out I had a twin as an adult? So weird! And then to think if she had been sent to another country, so even if we did find each other, we wouldn't be able to communicate.

Having never visited the South, I'm taken off guard by the walking contradiction. Korean man. Southern drawl. Compelled to impose, I ask if he likes the area and what part of the South is he from.

He whispers, "Ah don't like livin' in Savannah much. Ah'm not stayin' in the South much longer. Ah wouldn't mind movin next to kin." With the black felt cowboy hat now in hand, the man pushes the elevator UP button. I suspect he doesn't like to advertise his distaste for the South. The thought of being heard in public probably makes him nervous.

"I can imagine," I reply empathetically, wondering how the heck this young guy got stuck down there. If we were truly orphans—with deceased parents, then sure, move us as far away from our homeland as possible—if that's what these people think is best. But if we're not orphans, what right does the agency have to totally dislocate us from the possibility of ever reuniting with our family in the future? How could an agency displace this guy to such a far-off rural location? Even in regions around my community, covert racism and subtle insulting assumptions against minorities still exist. My sister and her ex-husband (originally from Kenya) were greeted with dirty stares even around our area just for wanting to use the restroom in one of the shops. The only reason they were allowed inside was that they were accompanied by one of their Caucasian patients.

"Unknown" birds are not made welcome in certain American diners, rural towns, and even in the cities. We just don't go there. But to live in the South as the lone Korean kid where extreme "right-winged" political parties and religious sects thrive, with no place to fly off to, must be so isolating. The only way to survive, to my knowledge, would be to *become* the surroundings, at least to the best of our ability. Assimilate or be destroyed.

"Yore sister told me yore a writer. 'Spose you read Katy Rawbinsin's book?" he asks, breaking me out of my concern.

"Katy, who?"

"Katy Rawbinsin. She wrote A Single Square Pictha."

"No, I haven't," I say, remembering the day at Walden's bookstore where I almost bought Ms. Robinson's memoir. I even skimmed the paperback over but slipped it back on the shelf since keeping no cash on me. Maybe I just wasn't ready to face my own adoption. Reading about the adoptee could possibly force me to speculate on the discrepancies in my own life. Ignorance, in my case, has been bliss.

"Ah fergot to tell your sis to read it. The agency lied."

The elevator doors open, and a full load of adoptees exit; each of us headed for the buses outside for the dinner and show. Amidst the activity, I tell the young Korean guy I'll look for the book.

He waits for the traffic to trickle down and then moseys inside the elevator. "Well. Ah gotta git. Gotta warsh up." He tells me before the door closes. "See yew tonaht or tomarr!"

"Okay! Thanks. Pleased to meet you. Maybe I'll see you tonight!" I smile and wave, but at the same time, a red flag goes up. When I get inside the next elevator, I send it straight to the top where the vendors are and pick up a copy of Katy's book. Then on the way to the temple for dinner, I ignore everyone around me like a hermit, skimming the book from a more critical perspective. Usually, I trust authorities more so than myself, yet many passages force me to question, again, the motives of adoption agencies.

Katy writes how, when she first arrived, the workers took her belongings and clothes and told her to select pants and a top from a crumpled mound they had on the floor. Even after writing her story, I sense that she's still oblivious to the deceptive acts made by the orphanage. I ponder another crazy thought, alert, now, to the possibility of lies. Are these glorified American orphanages purposely kept run-down and the children intentionally dressed in ratty clothes so the agency can collect endorsements from Americans who feel sorry for the "orphans"? Is this an advertising and fund-raising scheme? Where does the money go?

The adoption agency told Katy's adoptive mother that she had been abandoned at birth and left at the doorsteps of a police station and that she grew up in an orphanage. A lie. Her grandmother had hidden a bundle of photos in her backpack, painting a different story. Evidence showed she came from a comfortable and even well-to-do Korean family. Her well-dressed mother and grandmother took her to the airport and sent her off. Her mother wore a tailored tweed blazer over a long black dress with a turquoise scarf stylishly tied around her neck. Her black hair was groomed in good taste, and she appeared as if she could afford to keep her daughter had she been given the right type of counseling—counseling that encouraged rather than dissuaded.

When Katy's adoptive mother found the hidden photos, she contacted the agency, but they stood by their lies, and still today, no one has ever thought to suspect the agency of foul play. The question of whether "adoption is the right thing to do" has not been scrutinized. The photos in Katy's memoir prompted a suspicion against these businesses. Could these "godly" folks really be greedy folks? The thought is ludicrous! I've never given this much thought before.

Katy's book tells how the social worker did agree to look for her Korean father since her file showed that he had attempted to locate her at the agency. And at their reunion, He revealed that he had tried to reach her for the past two decades. On Katy's second attempt to find her Korean mother a year later at the same agency, a different social worker (without a Korean accent) treated Katy abruptly and even chided her. Again, the social worker said she could make copies of certain papers but not any information on her mother and that any contact Katy made with her Korean mother needed to be through the agency. The social worker closed and removed the birth records from Katy's hands, claiming to protect her Korean mother's privacy.

Is "protecting birth parents" a standard line used to deter adoptees from investigating further? It's been implied that our Korean parents don't want us to contact them. This may be true, but it should be the responsibility of the parents to tell us—so that we know this statement is true rather than hearsay. Unless the child is truly an orphan, both birth mother and father should write affidavits affirming that they truly no longer want to have rights to and further contact with their children, and then state the reason for their decision so we know they have not been coerced. Potential parents (of loss) also need to be aware of the not so glamorized and glorified adoptee stories. This way, the parents won't be solely influenced by agencies who are paid to send children overseas. The so-called "abandoned" children (as claimed by facilitators) will have proof that we have not been a victim of agencies' exploitation.

A Taste of Temple

The religion of the future will be a cosmic religion. It should transcend personal God and avoid dogma and theology. Covering both the natural and the spiritual, it should be based on a religious sense arising from the experience of all things natural and spiritual as a meaningful unity. Buddhism answers this description... If there is any religion that could cope with modern scientific needs, it would be Buddhism.
—Albert Einstein

Four hundred or more adoptees, along with photographers, are taken by buses to the Kwansmunsa Temple. At the premises, we walk in a long line of foot traffic around the Seoul Arts Center, which is a performance building on the large property. The open blue sky calms resembles an ocean of peaceful energy, and it welcomes us. *There she is.* I see the shrine ahead. The colorful Kwansmunsa Temple shines amidst the city landscape. It's a house-size building frosted with immaculate paint. Each of the four walls is colored in dizzying patterns. Massive symbols and art painted in turquoise, red, cobalt blue, black, pink, and white cover the ceiling in a flowery pattern. A black roof curls up at four corners, exposing layers of thick, wooden aqua-colored beams, like the ample ruffles and frills under a lacy square dancing dress.

I watch the crowd, looking for my twin sister. On the steps leading into the temple, adoptees scramble in and out of the premises, many shooting snapshots of the multiple white statuettes of Buddha adorning a red-and-gold sidewall.

Where is my sister? Being of Korean ethnicity, each and every participant could pass for my relative. In a corner on the left side, I think I see Jenette. The black hair is familiar as it flows straight down the back and frizzy from the humidity. She's facing one of the two main altars sitting side by side, one holding a photo of the Bodhisattva of Compassion and the other of Bodhisattva of Power. I prance over, happy to have finally found my twin, and tap her on the shoulder. When she turns around, I realize the gal is not my twin.

"Oh, hi," I say, pretending to know her and that I meant to get her attention. "Pretty cool, huh?"

The gal grins, but it's awkward. *Oops.* I pretend to be absorbed with the scenery for a while, then gradually twist around like a dork to search the moving crowd for my sister again. There is so much to look at. Ornamental altars, surrounded by symbols and art, call out for my attention. Buddhist Guardians and Eastern angels meant to terrify the greedy adorn the ceiling and then spring off an iridescent hardwood floor in fiery passion. Fruit and flower arrangements are offered to appease the clergymen. As modest as the gifts appear, they're prepared with the greatest care and presented with the best of possible intentions. Offerings, a symbol of a worshipper's humility, obedience, prayer, and gratitude, play an integral part in contemplation. A Buddhist's awareness of truth suggests that if anything, no matter how small, is not respected, it loses its value.

Where's Jenette? Seeing so many black-haired individuals, I'm close to giving up when I pass a glimpse of my sister's stupid big black camera. The whirl and whiz noise it makes when she focuses in and out confirms my suspicion. Everyone else is holding tiny silver digital electronics that fit nicely into white-collar shirt pockets, akin to modern-day pocket protectors.

There she is. Geez! I can't lose her now that I know she's got her dorky camera with her. (But it's better than mine. At least with her taking pictures with it, I don't have to pull out the Wal-Mart disposals from my purse).

This time, I tip-toe over to the corner she's standing against, next to a black-and-white photo of a Buddhist priest (who achieved enlightenment at age forty-one, inspiring him to bring Buddhism and form Korea's Chentae's order) and call her name.

An identical face swerves around. *Whew, it's her!*

"Where have you been?" Next to the saint, Jenette instantly gripes, "I've had the camera the entire time. I'm tired of taking pictures. It's your turn."

Not wanting to be caught dead or alive with my sister's camera, I avoid taking it and keep my hands safely stuck inside my dress pockets.

"What the heck?" My sister is able to read my body language. She knows I'm snubbing her request. "You expect *me* to take pictures during this entire trip?"

"No. I'll take a few. Just not now."

"Don't tell me." Her eyes narrow. "You don't even know how to use the camera?

"Of course, I do. I just don't want to do it now."

"All you gotta do is push this button," my sister says, agitation growing.

"I'll do it later."

"What? You're not going to photograph the temple? There are no Buddhist temples in the U.S.!" She scoffs. "And you're not going to take photos of this one?"

"I will. Just not now. I want to wait until the adoptees clear out."

"What is wrong with you? You're not even going to take pictures. This is our first trip back. We might never get to come here again. And you've decided you're not going to take pictures! Something is seriously wrong with you."

"Whatever." I scowl at my twin. "What the heck is wrong with you?"

"Duh. I'm the one taking all the pictures." She shrugs.

"Maybe Buddha doesn't want his picture taken. Have you thought of that?" I say, aware that the comment is utterly childish.

"Oh, my God. Well, if you're not going to take the camera. Here." She fights with a large SwapMeet duffel bag and lugs out her camcorder, then pushes it toward me. "Take the camcorder."

I swallow hard and wish that I had taken her camera. "Fine," I concede.

"This is for both of us. Not just for me. So do a good job. Keep it steady," she carps, totally reading me. She knows that I'm just too lazy to be bothered.

I study the box and play dumb. "How do I turn this thing on, anyway?"

Jenette sighs deeply then pushes a few buttons. The whole thing lights up, and suddenly I can see the floor through a window. Raising and moving it around a bit, it records the monks during their meditation. This entire time, we've been arguing in front of a few locals kneeling at the foot of the Eastern saints, meditating upon peace and love. "Now. Whatever you see on the screen is what you'll be recording," my twin instructs, a little too demeaning.

"Duh. I know. I'm not an idiot," I state through gritted teeth and stomp off before she nags at me more.

"Whatever!"

We've been oblivious to the fact that we've been standing in front of the monks and interrupting their soft chant with our obnoxious foreign wrangling. Our disruption could be compared to if foreigners were having a fight in the middle of a church service prayer. Here in the East, heaven on earth is supposed to be attained by meditation. Chanting is a loving internal offering a monk gives to the Universe for the betterment of humankind. "Being" in a peaceful place can help to dissolve the "three poisons" consisting of greed, anger, and foolishness. The temple is a sacred place where an adherent is able to release the mindful tensions of past resentments and future worries (releasing in the East is the same as forgiveness is in the West).

I can't decide what to focus on inside the glistening building. The mix of colors painted into symbolic patterns on the ceiling fascinates me. It's as if I've been transported to an ancient time. As a child, I wasn't allowed to explore Buddhism. It was considered, by my parents, treading on treacherous territory. Fortunately, by the time my adoptive Dad had reached his late sixties, he expanded his belief system to include Metaphysics, gaining consideration for every culture and belief system. Therefore, we've been able to explore world religions together.

Each religion and philosophy use symbols that represent something meaningful, and everyone believes in the same God otherwise perceived as "Source" or "Force." The East believes God is an *internal* force that extends around us; the West believes God is an *external* force that is over and beyond the clouds. The East meditates or *listens* for God's grace; the West prays or *asks* for God's grace. If we were to reduce the Source, both sides pretty much agree that love is God, and God is love. Compassion is the doorway.

The Eastern costumes are made to scare away evil intruders or ghosts. God is perceived as attainable within and a source of love, light, and inspiration. Meditation gives access to the divine spirit so that, by being in tune with it, we can manifest our concern and compassion out into the world. Sadly, the beautiful symbolism and peaceful Buddhist and wise Confucius connotations have been ignored and twisted to appear evil by fearful imperialists.

Eventually, I bump into my sister again and play dumb so that she won't trust me with her camcorder again. "Hey.

Jenette," I ask, sticking the camcorder out toward her. "How do I turn this thing off?"

"Duh." She sighs heavily. "With the same button, I used to turn it on." She grabs it from my light grasp and snaps it off. "Like this."

"Hey, how am I supposed to know that?" I ask, watching her stuff the thing back into the bag as I follow her out of the temple. We take ten minutes to locate our shoes amidst the piles and mass movement. Eventually, we slip on our shoes, then stomp down the steps onto the cement walkway below, and blend in with everyone headed for the buffet dinner.

Jenette suddenly bursts into elation. "Oh, my God, Janine." She flounces my hair and wiggles my shoulders. "I gotta tell you! There's another set of twins I found!"

We somehow always manage to end things on a positive note. I think it's in our blood.

Our Plates are Full

"I value seeking sustenance from the Mother."
—Lao-tzu

Immediately after the West meets East visit to the Kwansmunsa Temple, the group will be treated to a lunch by the adherents. Jenette and I find Christina, and the three of us laugh our way downstairs to the basement for the buffet. Once the large group is seated, event officials greet us in celebration. A bottle of champagne is opened, and a cake waits to be cut into pieces for dessert. At the front, a man with a microphone welcomes us, translating messages from Korean to English. When he begins, a woman inches up to the edge of the platform and, in a whisper, interrupts the spokesman. I can't see her, but I hear that she is too shy to walk on stage. It's hard to get the group's attention at first, but eventually, we quiet down. I can't see the woman, but I know she is upset, speaking Korean to whoever will listen. A minute goes by while the translator listens to her, then interprets bits and pieces for us into a microphone.

"She is looking for her lost child . . ."

Multiple gasps erupt from the crowd of four hundred or so. The entire room implodes with wonder. Adoptees lock eyes with friends sitting next to and across from us, taken aback at the idea.

"A daughter . . ."

"Oh, my gosh, Christina. It could be you!" Jenette exclaims. For the first time during our vacation, Christina isn't laughing. Same as everyone else, she suddenly appears solemn at the thought.

Sitting on picnic-style benches, women wonder: *Is it me? It might be me. What does it feel like to have a mother look at me with an identical sparkle and a knowing smile?* The thought is intriguing.

"Her daughter has a birthmark," interprets the man for the troubled woman.

I try to remember where my birthmarks might be. *Let's see, one on the palm of my left hand, one on my neck, one on my face.* The women around show birthmarks to old and new friends. It's as if we're living a fairy-tale, hoping that the shoe fits. In our case, we're wondering if the birthmark is in the right spot. Will there be a happily-ever-after tale to tell for one of us?

"On her shoulder," the translator says.

Christina, Jenette, and I examine our own and then each other's shoulders.

"Wait," Christina whispers to Jenette. "What's that?" She's pointing to a dot the size of a sugar ant. "It could be you!"

I squint to make out my sister's tiny dot. "Nah," I conclude, "it's just an age spot."

We women pull at the collars of nearby friends, looking for the mark. Even the guys help us look. By now, the activity room is filled with noise as we examine our shoulders for some sort of mark. My tan shoulders are spotless—not a speck of dust—just moist from the swelling heat. And so are the gals sitting close to me.

The man at the podium repeats the woman's plea, "Her daughter was born in 1982."

Jenette squeals, "Oh, my gosh, Christina. It could really be you!"

This arouses calculations and confusion. I feel like a dummy while recalculating my age with the help of my fingers. Being in this situation makes me doubt everything I've ever known about myself. *Nope. Couldn't be me. Too old.*

"She may be twenty now."

"Oh, my gosh!" My sister squeals, almost ripping away our young friend's shirt collar, while the monks watch against the walls. "Christina, it could be you!"

The female adoptees in the room conjecture the age given to us by agencies. What if we weren't born on the date recorded on our paperwork? We wonder if the inquiring mother has her information right. It looks as if most every female adoptee, regardless of age, speculates: *Is it me?* Not trusting my math, I calculate Jenette's and my age again with the help of my fingers, even though we're years older than the mother's displaced daughter. We couldn't possibly be the child she is looking for. *There are two of us!* (I think the mother would have remembered giving birth to two babies.)

After a while, the room's noise expires into quietude. To everyone's wonder, no one runs to the front, bearing the mark that belongs to the missing daughter. An awkward silence follows the room's depleted adrenaline rush. The monks and officials are at a loss with what to do with the bereft woman. They shrug and nod empathetically at each other. The adoptees whisper amongst small groups about the mother and her displaced daughter.

Amidst the abrupt silence within our small group, everyone waits, wondering what's next. It takes a few minutes before the cafeteria noise resumes into loud talk again amongst the conjoined lunch tables, and it seems as if everyone already forgets the woman's concern. In our small group, Christina picks up a Korean beer bottle, scrutinizes it, and then laughs. "Oh, my Gawd. They've given us beer to drink. Inside a Buddhist Temple of all places." *Hilarious!* We smirk at the peculiar situation.

Anyway, I think our plates are full. Many of us have been sent to superb nests with professional working parents who encouraged and paid for college educations (although Jenette and I were on our own in this department). We grew up surrounded by the best of families—like magnificent trumpeter swans. Why would adoptees want to revert to the past when there's a risk of non-acceptance and misunderstandings? By now, many of us are professionals, managing family, career, extended education, finances, and maybe even hobbies, coupled with our adoptive parents' influence and belief system. I'd hate to tell the mourning mother, whether she's wonderful or wretched, that many of us haven't ever felt the need to look for her. Many of us are too busy working, trying to scratch out a living. My mind wavers back and forth over, finding my own mother.

I've had a pretty decent life filled with abundance and opportunities, successes, and failures. The love I've received from my American family has always been considered superior, and it has shaped and influenced my sister and me into believing the love from our Korean family is of no significance. And so we never felt the desire to look for them. I would have hated to see my adoptive parents go without children. Now, Dad's in his mid-seventies. He tells Jenette and me that if it weren't for the two of us, he'd be stuck in a coop without kin to check up on him. To think of him potentially without a flock makes me heartsick. I've always been satisfied to be his loyal daughter. Yep. As much as I hate to be the messenger, our plates are most certainly full. By now, we've adjusted to the lives given to us when children.

Regaining their composure, the women slide Gap and Guess T-shirt collars back into place. The mother covers her face with trembling hands, avoiding everyone's eyes, and runs out of the cafeteria, embarrassed for making such a shameful scene.

At dinner, there is a mini quandary and a little laughter over whether we, adoptees, should eat with forks or chopsticks.

Most use both. How to grasp the eating utensils properly? I even laugh at myself for my own clumsiness. After the rest of the celebratory talk and the failed attempt for a reunion, we socialize at the tables and go back to examining the unfamiliar Korean dishes, forgetting, alas, the roving mother of loss.

After lunch, Christina is still in good spirits. Jenette and I follow her out of the cafeteria, and we merge into the stream of adoptees. We've become loud and obnoxious again.

When we pass an older Korean woman standing against a wall dressed in a shiny traditional hanbok, Christina backs up and changes into a sweet Korean girl. She curtsies, and with an unusually high-pitched voice, sings, "Annyeong-haseyo!" (Hello)

The woman smiles.

"Bus?" Christina asks.

The woman looks confused and shakes her head 'no.'

Christina metamorphoses into an American teenager: Using gestures resembling hands on a steering wheel, she inquires again, only this time with a deep voice. "Bus? Bus?"

The Korean woman points us in the opposite direction.

Upon leaving the flow of traffic, Christina changes into a Korean girl once again, bowing and singing sweetly, "Gamsa-hamnida!" (Thank you!)

My twin and I trail behind our young teen friend, clutching her shoulders as if we're her blind ducklings, knowing all the while that we planned to have fun on this trip.

At the end of the hall, she hits an impasse with multiple doors. Jenette chirps, "Which one do we choose?"

"Yeah!" I peep, "Which one do we choose?"

Christina slowly opens the left side door, and a loud creak resonates from old hinges.

"What's inside?" Jenette and I ask together. "The bus?"

"Oh, my Gawd!" Christina explodes into hilarity. "It's the bathroom!"

Man's Begotten Son

On a lonely hilltop, away from the distant mist,
A golden dragon stands, staring with
Dreams that fade and die in the bright West.[14]
—Bruce Lee

The afternoon trip to the Blue House arrives quickly. Friday afternoon, four hundred adoptees are divided by age and taken onto grand tour buses for a visit to Cheong Wa Dae, South Korea's official presidential retreat. Each passport has been verified by security before leaving.

There is so much chaos attempting to get onto the buses that by the time I catch up with Jenette, I find she's squished between a set of male twins and laughing hysterically. I end up finding a seat a few past hers and scoot toward the bus window so someone can move in. Several individuals pass, shuffling along the aisle and eyeing the back. After a few minutes, an adoptee dressed in a white oxford shirt and black slacks eventually stops and scoots in next to me. He is maybe my age and resembles one of the Korean pop stars from many of the airport advertisements I had seen, mostly due to shoulder-length hair touching his neck—a style not common in the states at the moment. We give each other a polite smile and wait. The bus is so rowdy and on the verge of overflowing that I am reminded of high school. This time, thank goodness, we're in the company of fellow adoptees, strangers connected by ethnic blood, making us Seoul sisters and brothers. No one here is going to shout the infamous chant against Asians: "go back to where you came from! You don't belong here!" All of us *are* back to where we came from! And it feels great!

Finally, the buses leave one by one, producing a train-like processional out of the hotel parking lot, each one headed in one direction: toward the governmental premises. I look out the window and notice a few individuals in black T-shirts waving a banner that could have something to do with a protest.

"Who are the people with black T-shirts on?" I ask the stranger, scooting back so he can look past me and out the window to the bright street below.

"Oh. Them." He tells me in a European accent. "They're considered the 'bad' guys."

"Bad guys?"

"They're adoptees against inter-country adoption."

I can't believe it and have to ask, "And they're adoptees? I've never heard of an adoptee against adoption. We *are* adoption. We're the ones agencies recruit to speak *for* adoption!"

"Lots of adoptees are against adoption."

"They are?" The thought baffles me. They're sure well-hidden from public display. "But why?"

"Many believe separation from biological families is a violation of the most fundamental human rights. They don't want Korean children to suffer the same consequences, especially since the Korean War ended fifty years ago, and there's no reason for outside entities, such as agencies, to have such jurisdiction."

"Really? But I've always been trained to see my adoption as all good."

"I, for one, want to see inter-country adoption stopped here in Korea," the adoptee admits, to my astonishment.

Not really knowing what to say, I'm silent at his comment, too shocked at the thought of anyone against adoption. I'm also partially fascinated by his speech. I rarely get to talk with someone from Europe, so I'm a bit excited and wonder from which country he could be. Maybe Austria or France?

"I know this is not going to happen," the man continues. "Bringing awareness and education to adoptive parents concerning their Korean child is a must, even if only one child can be spared the fate that I went through in my childhood, then my life has been worthwhile."

"Why would you want it stopped?" I still can't comprehend the thought.

"I think there are major problems."

"Like what?"

He uses his fingers to count the reasons. "Access to accurate and correct information. Cooperation from the adoption services. Fair treatment. Non-exploitive help at hand, should adoptees seek their parents."

I nod, thinking back to my recent run-in with the post-adoption office in search of my own Korean family. I was just finding out for the first time that a run-in with them is like having a run-in with the law. He, on the other hand, appears to have studied the topic. I still feel unaware of the industry and in a state of surprise over it. This trip is the only time in our lives that we will look for our Korean family. After the voyage is over, we'll go back to living our normal everyday life without them and forget.

I'm awed by his immediate answers and tell him, "You're so aware of what's been going on."

"Adoption is my life."

I nod. "Yeah. Mine too, I guess. But I just never thought it was ever a big deal."

The driver shifts gears, and the engine of the bus roars over the crowded paved roads. In order to be heard, we have to shout. I watch Seoul's brick buildings and storefront windows fly by outside. The streets are full of people, but I also noticed the energy from the land of the morning calm. I have noticed they seem strangely void of children. Is it because agencies have been sending the little ones abroad privately and secretively?

Feeling compelled to ask, I break the silence, "Have you looked for your birth parents?"

"Social Welfare Services (SWS) never kept in touch with me. I tried to join their website and apply for a subscription, but my mail was never replied to. Eventually, this Korean woman responded and said that she had been back to the house where I was said to be found. Nobody can remember me being left there. What was particularly annoying is the fact that I didn't ask her to go look in the first place!"

"Man, that's rude."

"Social Welfare has changed their site to an all-Korean version, which for somebody like me who does not know any Korean, I perceive this to be a form of "lockout," which is really quite rude and uncalled for."

"Yeah. That doesn't make sense."

"If I wanted to find my parents, then I damn well would, and I would make it quite clear to SWS that was my real intention. As it happens, for the foreseeable future, I'm not."

The tour bus's processional turns left onto another street filled with restaurants and stores. Red, green, black, and white signs call out for our attention with sale prices and quality products, but we can't read any of the words. It's like going around blind and deaf in our hometown. So intrigued by this adoptee who ended up on the other side of the world from me, I break the silence once more. "But didn't you have a good life with your adoptive family?"

"What do you mean?" He asks.

"I mean, seems like anyone who had a good life doesn't really feel the need to look for their biological family . . . . What I'm trying to say is that I've always considered myself to be fortunate . . . Or too lucky to ever ask for more. So, didn't you feel lucky?"

"Not really."

"What do you mean?" I ask.

"My mom was different. She was neglectful. She used to hit me a lot, too."

"Oh my gosh, that's horrible! What about your dad? Did he know?"

"My father never hit me. When I think of my adoptive father and mother, I was really fearful of them. My father never hit me, but his voice roared at me, usually when I was ill. I became upset and started crying. I remember one year I had the flu, and I couldn't breathe. My father thought I was faking, and he yelled at me to stop coughing. I couldn't. The doctor came out and diagnosed the flu. My chest had seized."

"That's horrible! What kind of relationship do you have now?"

"My adoptive parents made life hard for me. I never loved my adoptive parents. Nor do I now. I miss my dad a bit. He died years ago. We only really started to get along in the last few months of his life."

"That's too bad. I'm sorry."

"As for my mom, I am glad that I will never see her again, and if I do, then it will be not before ten years or more has passed."

"I can understand your feeling. But why wouldn't you want to find your birth parents then?"

"It's plain and simple to me. I think of it this way. If my birth mom wanted me so much, she wouldn't have given me away or abandoned me in the first place. The fact that she did sends one clear signal. She was not interested in me from the beginning. Why would she be any more inquisitive about me thirty years later?"

"I don't know." By now, I quietly suspect his Korean mother could have been given the wrong type of counseling, similar to the others. How disgraceful.

"There are no words in the human language that my birth mother can express to take away the bitterness, the pain, and the hurt. The zest that my life should have been filled with was taken from me, and what remains is the husk, a tough, bitter, and angry one at that. Why on earth would I go searching for people I know are going to end up making more problems for me?"

I reflect on his words and his life. It seems so sad and cruel. I'm surprised at how open he is, but then we all have been during this trip. For many of us, it's the first time we've encountered other "unknown" birds. It's the first time we make up the majority instead of the lone minority. We're all in the same boat—or rather the same bus. Plus, we're talking with strangers. Tomorrow, we'll depart and never see each other again.

"My adoptive parents had a poor attitude, galactic ignorance, lack of education. They inflicted mental and physical abuse upon me, causing me to have much fear, distress, and loneliness while I was young."

"So, did you get any sort of support at all?"

He sneers and shakes his head no. "Between the ages of eleven and fifteen, I was a confused and strange child. If you had known me back then, I was really quite obnoxious and irritating. I always felt quite old for my age, and I blame this partly on my adoptive mother. Everything I did was carefully scrutinized. She and my adoptive father examined my actions around the dinner table. I'd dare not say anything. My mother took everything I said personally, and my father took her side."

"I actually can relate, I think," I say, but keep silent regarding the fact that at least I had a biological sibling to identify with.

"My spoken communication skills and social skills were really stunted in comparison to somebody my own age. Amongst my own peer group, I was verbally bullied, and I never fit in with anyone. I was just a 'stupid chink,' 'nip,' or 'yellow-belly bastard'! One time in school, a senior came over and ordered that I clean his shoes because I looked like a shoe-shine boy in one of his grandfather's old photographs."

"Man, that's horrible!" I can't even imagine the man I'm talking with having any trouble communicating. He's so articulate, so educated.

"One of my school teachers thought it pertinent to remind the pupils that Koreans ate dogs. My parents surprisingly reacted quickly. When the teacher was questioned, she merely stated, 'We as Europeans have a right to know what his habits and lifestyle entails, and this is an integral part of *his* culture.'"

"Man, that sucks," I say, remembering the same accusation being thrown around at the school I had attended.

"School was the best and worst years of my younger life; it allowed me to escape the atmosphere at home but thrust me into the unwanted limelight of racial cruelty that still shakes me to the core today."

"Seems like you've learned to work past it."

He nods. "Oddly, I was polite and respectful, but when I look back, this was not respect. It was fear. The mental and physical abuse from both my parents was one of the biggest hurdles whilst growing up. Nobody in school understood why I was so strange. I think I must have switched off and gone into a daze."

It's hard to imagine his story. But then, again, it also seems eerily familiar. Because of the conference, we now, at least, know that we're not the only Asian and the only adoptee in the world.

"For a long time, I never liked 'Chinese' people. I found them embarrassing. I could hear my adoptive mother in the distance, remarking, 'But you're part of their people. How can you dislike them so much? Why don't you want to be them?'" Her ignorance and stupidity at mistaking one ethnic group for another is almost laughable in the present day, but her blunt and ignorant opinions made it difficult for me to want to be with anyone from the Far East."

Our conversation reminds me of the issues within my own life. Thank goodness the human spirit is resilient and willing to let go of injustices. Children, especially, have a magical way of just bouncing back. Still, part of our past stays with us and tends to show up once in a while, in one way or another.

The "unknown" adoptee speaks again with an unidentifiable European accent. And every time he does, it catches me off guard. "I used to cringe when a Chinese guy came on the TV with a karate suit on," he tells me, "because I knew that the next day in school, everybody just equated me to that stereotypical image."

"Yeah," is what I say while picturing the clichéd Asian nerd/exchange student—the only image of Asians shown on the silver screen. It's so trite!

"When people made racist comments about my appearance, my mother and father just told me to ignore it. Sometimes they even laughed, supposedly for me."

"So what do you think should be done?" I wonder aloud, tremendously shocked at this side of adoption, not so glamorous, not so glorious.

"The selection process for parents adopting children from Korea needs to be improved quite significantly. One of the notions clear in my mind is that if parents are rejected for adoption in their own indigenous country, why should the couple be allowed to adopt a child from another country with any less legal restrictions?"

"That's true."

"This is surely a major contradiction and something that needs to be addressed at the United Nations level. To provide adequate protection for children, minors, and babies from the clutches of people who are not fit to be parents in the first place, we need a standardized procedure enforced by strict international law. Otherwise, the aim and the eventual goal contradicts itself—that is to provide the best possible start."

I'm silent and filling with anger, feeling irresponsible for being so naive of the laws that govern us, adoptees. Meanwhile, the world outside flies by without notice.

The composed male adoptee interrupts the silence between us. "Adoptive parents have a huge responsibility in bringing up a child of a different ethnicity. The child's heritage and roots should not be taken lightly or anecdotally. It is, after all, the other half of the child that needs balance and attention. Otherwise, the child grows up deficient, in some ways, giving way to future problems."

"I agree with you there. So you don't believe the line adoption agencies use, claiming they're saving 'orphans'?"

"My adoptive parents used to say they took me out of Korea because they knew it was a better start for me in my life. That's just total rubbish! In the late 1970s, the nation I grew up in had unemployment reaching over 3 million! The national inflation was over seventy-eight percent! The eighties were, in effect, the morning after the sugar-coated period in the economic history akin to the depression in the USA in the early 30s."

Hmm. I mull over the situation while this most unfortunate adoptee continues his point. "This argument that adoptive parents commonly and freely spout irritates me intensely; it's merely a poor assumption. My father used to boast that the education system was the best in the world. In fact, it hasn't been the best education system in the world for the past 30 years! Sure, places like Ivy League colleges and many of the public schools/grammar schools are good places to attend, but after my father had left the army, he was unemployed for four years! This had an imploding effect on my relationship with them in my earlier years and on my adoptive parents' marriage. What is the likelihood of me being able to attend one of those high-class institutions? I'm considered a second-class citizen in the West! At least in Korea, I wouldn't have been so obviously isolated as an outcast based on first impressions. A life of poverty is not the only choice here in the East. Any one of us could have become the President of South Korea if we so chose. Instead, we get the blessing of 'forever families' who proudly state they are 'color blind' and dismiss our ethnic heritage as if it's worth nothing."

Wow is all I can think. I'm stumped and speechless.

The bus finally stops, and we're given permission to exit. Too busy talking and socializing, I don't pay attention to the pearly white gates trimmed with gold or the guards dressed in military uniforms. I barely notice the beautiful round spa-size water fountain, the cement statues of families, and the crane, like an angel, stretching its neck toward the sun. As we stand to leave and then hobble down the bus steps onto South Korea's Presidential grounds, this man's comments stay with me. I lose the potential Korean star in the shuffle and never see him again; however, I will never forget his reasoning and the story behind it.

As Nature Made Us

I believe in God, only I spell it Nature.
—Frank Lloyd Wright

"Oh, my God. Janine. There are s-o-o many parties going on. I've made the arrangements. All you gotta do is follow my lead. You've got to enjoy yourself. Get wasted. Let loose!" My sister hollers at me from the doorway of the cramped bathroom. On the opposite side, I'm relaxing on the hotel bed. For the past hour, she's dominated the bathroom in preparation for the last of many parties going on around the city. I hear the blow-dryer hum a low tone in the background, and I think she's finally done. Getting ready for the evening comes easy for her, especially due to the straightening perm she got at a Korean-American salon. She only needs to wash and go. My hair, on the other hand, has grown into one feathery mess.

My sister applies make-up with a steady hand. By now, she's got the right formula to fit her needs. "What are you going to wear?" she hollers from the other side of the wall. "You've got to wear something cute. Hey, why don't you wear the new skirt you bought before the trip? It makes you look totally hot!"

Always interested in true life stories, I'm reading the book I had brought along on the trip that now seems so jarringly similar to what I call interracial adoptees' "life swap," "identity theft," and "trading spaces." It's called *As Nature Made Him: The Boy who was Raised as a Girl*. The little boy was made to play with girl toys, wear dresses, and even forced to act like a girl—someone he wasn't—caused by a messed-up circumcision. The boy's plight plays in my mind over and over, a recording that won't stop. Not only is he an outcast at school and in the neighborhood, he just felt "wrong." For twenty-five years, the case of John/Joan was called a medical triumph—proof that a child's gender identity could be changed—and thousands of "sex reassignments" were performed based on this example. The fact that the boy felt "wrong" his entire life was ignored by the medical journals and the community based on the doctor's reports—a doctor with his own agenda who wanted to prove nurture wins over nature. *Hmm. Just like adoptions have been labeled social triumphs.*

From the bathroom, my sister is still working magic with her long slippery black hair and spouting off the night's plans.

All I can concentrate on is the boy who was raised a girl. As an adult, the victim pointed out that his parents felt guilty as if the whole thing was their fault. Defending his parents, he stated that the mistakes they made had been out of kindness, love, and desperation. "When you're desperate, you don't necessarily do the right things." He reported that the childhood transgender experiment was like brainwashing.[15] Tragically, at age 38, the victim committed suicide. The press placed little emphasis on the sexual reassignment and instead blamed "bad investments, marital problems, and his brother's death two years earlier."[16]

"Janine. Janine! What are you going to wear?"

"What?" I snap out of my daze to the blare of my sister's nagging.

"What are you going to wear to the parties?"

"What parties?"

"Haven't you been listening?" She pops her head out of the bathroom. Black, brown, and auburn hair is dried and straightened, and her eyes are smeared in Smoky Black Magic

Eyeliner. Divine Wine lipstick and Innocent Pink blush enhance her face. "Or are you spacing out again?"

Ugh. I've got to stop mulling this over. It's driving me insane!

She disappears, but I can hear her inhale deeply and then exhale, annoyed. "Listen to me, Janine. We are going to party like it's 1999. You better get ready now! Let's try to find the Belgium twins. I've heard about them. But I haven't met them yet. We've got to find two identical faces."

"Now, where exactly are we going?"

Jenette darts out of the bathroom and throws me a kelly green sleeveless top and chocolate brown skirt from out of my opened suitcase. "Wear this with your brown boots." She's all dolled up in black. I know she's going to wear her fading Italian leather closed-toe shoes with the outfit cuz she always does. She turns around and models the dress for me, but I've seen it on her a thousand times already. She stares at herself in the mirror over the dresser.

Barely getting out of the covers, I find a black top from my suitcase and attempt to pull it out from under the mess of clothes.

"I'm wearing black," she tells me, snapping the wadded top from my hands.

"Hey, but I wanted to wear black." Because we're identical twins, attempting to look as different as possible, I know that I'm not supposed to wear black when she is.

"No. I'm wearing black!" She jams her selection for me into my hands. "I've made plans. We're going to find the Belgium twins at the dinner. Then we're going to find Christina at the after-Gathering party. Then we're meeting the French twins at the French café for after-party drinks. Then we're going to meet the Seattle twins and follow everyone to Karaoke!"

She snatches a green bottle of Korean beer from the fridge, then looks at her watch set at Seoul time (mine is still set at Seattle's). After taking a sip of beer, she shakes her head at my sluggish moves. Her hair flows comparable to that silky smooth

Korean shampoo commercial. "Will you hurry up? We gotta get out of here!"

I surrender, scoot out of bed, and settle into the bathroom where I find my expired hair products from the old days—during my twenties. I don't know which bottle to start with. Getting my hair right is a new problem in Seoul, where the air sears the skin, and the sun dries the tresses. My heavy, coarse hair is a frizzy mess. After coaxing and teasing for an hour, it ends up a massive lion's mane. I cough my way out of the fumed and clammy bathroom, my hair feathered back resembling an odd bird, saturated with lightweight products made particularly for swans.

My twin scans my hair front and back and frowns after her examination. "You still haven't done your hair! Hurry up! Fix it so we can go!"

At a Gathering party, my sister sits at a table surrounded by guys and gals, and she's making the entire group laugh. She is able to draw the attention of many people as if she's the queen of the colony—the vivacity of the party. Her social Gemini side includes befriending everyone, especially our young friend Christina, who is thirteen years younger and has the character trait of a hilarious "old soul." We've taken Christina in as our own Seoul sister during The Gathering. Both she and my sister make surprisingly intuitive counselors to guys and gals they meet. I, on the other hand, encompass the Gemini mental energy. I'm so engrossed in isolated thought, I can barely stand myself. Put Jenette and me together (our curiosity and our interest in people), and eventually, we're able to analyze and pinpoint the origin of most relationship problems. We're so interested in humanity that we find everyone's story intriguing—fascinating, something to learn from! Sometimes, life can be much more insightful *with* drama! Without challenges, life might be boring, stagnant. The way we see it, identifying and facing problems, is an opportunity for humanity to advance to a level of acceptance and compassion—or Tao Te Ching (The Classical Way of Integrity).

After what feels like hours of wandering the floor like a walking android, I find a vacant corner to watch from. The smoke-filled room pervades us like a hot steam bath. Thick vapor from dry ice fills every empty space. The latest techno music plays at full blast onto multiple speakers above the cement floor. Spotlights shine down, swing around, and then, in various directions, spring off walls and dancing people. With arms flying and heads bopping, the partying adoptees look like they're bouncing on a full-size trampoline. The music reverberates and pulsates into the modern couches and sitting areas. We have to shout to be heard, and even then, we can barely hear one another.

From the dead center of the dance floor, I spot my sister emerge like Catwoman out of the haze of dry ice that hangs in low clouds. She marches across the floor to me, clasping another Korean beer bottle in her left hand. Her other hand clenches a cigarette. *Hmm. I didn't know she smoked.*

"Hey, when did you start smoking?" I scream over the hammering music.

She hollers back, "I always have to smoke when I drink."

"Oh."

She inhales a drag, then blows out through the corner of her mouth. After that, she takes a swig of beer and swallows hard. "Beer and cigarettes go hand in hand. You know, like the yin and the yang."

I nod and cross my arms as if I know what she's referring to, although I was never able to smoke a cigarette accurately.

She turns around, faces the crowd with me, and points her bottle toward the activity. "God, Janine. You see that girl?"

"Which one?"

"That one—with black hair."

I scan the crowd. Hundreds of girls are flailing around on the dance floor with lucid arms akin to rag dolls. Most of them have black hair. Many have brown highlights. Only a few have auburn.

And one has blond. Guys are intermixed in the crowd. "What girl?"

"That girl." My sister screams at me and points her green beer bottle to a tall, younger gal, beating her lanky body to the lyrics of a Black Eyed Peas song. The lead singer, Fergie, is singing, "I wonder if I take you home, would you still be in love, baby. In love, baby."

The girl continues to collide, glide, and gyrate her backside against a large guy, who is wearing a silver metallic shirt and white pants. The upbeat hip-hop song, "Don't Phunk with my Heart," inspires her determined, dirty, and flirty movements. After Fergie sings, "would you still be in love, baby," a deep male voice raps, "Girl, you know you got me. You got me."

My sister watches from the sidelines. "She is such a slut!"

"What? Why?"

"I've seen her flirting with all the guys. She's with that solitaire group."

"You mean solidarity group," I yell at the top of my lungs over the dance music, "It's made up of adoptees who live in Seoul. I heard they're attempting to stop the selling of Korean babies, but whoever is in control of the industry—both governments or the agencies or all—want this group to remain immobilized, and no one takes them seriously. No one asks them to speak at adoption panels, summits, and whatnot."

I watch the girl glide her backside up and down against the guy a second time. "She's from a solidarity group—not solitaire."

"Whatever." My sister drinks from the bottle and then points to the gal again. "Look! Did you see that? She's a slut."

"What?"

"She's getting w-a-a-y too close! He's married with kids!"

"How do you know?"

"Guys just seem to open up to me. They tell me stuff." My sister glares into the active crowd, eyes locked on the female. By now, the gal is thumping her hips and facing the man at eye level. Then she wiggles downward into a squatting position. Once at his navel, she shoots back up. The next thing we know, she's fiddling with his shirt buttons. "What the fu—do you see that?" My sister shouts, dropping her cigarette butt and smashing it into the cement floor with an aged Italian shoe.

"See what?"

"She's unbuttoning his shirt!" My sister barks, agitated at the thought.

"She is?" I say, detached, not wanting to get involved.

My sister clutches my arm, leaving a red impression, spouting obscenities at the same time. "She's trying to fuck him on the dance floor! I swear. That is so disgusting! He better not fall for it. Women can be s-o-o manipulative. I'm going over there and kick her ass." With her right hand balled into a tight fist, my twin (mother of two children—one a teenage son) barges toward the dancers before I can stop her.

I cringe at the thought of having to back my sister up and wrestle this girl. Typically, Jenette and I try to find humor in almost everything. We rarely take life so seriously. If we do get offended, it generally has to do with racist incidents, such as when we're treated with contempt due to our ethnicity. Even though I'm pretty good at detecting bullies, I haven't gotten in a fight since high school, and even then, I only loosely passed a few rude comments at a girl (I called "the bitch") for making fun of the aroma wafting through the school halls originating from the "What's Cooking" Class. One of my Filipino friends had made a national dish, and "the bitch" complained the school smelled like dog food because of it. So "the bitch," and I ended up shooting off rants against each other in the middle of the cafeteria. We stopped when a friend from the crowd interrupted our spew by jumping up and down (as if she was going to pee her pants) and pointed to our shoes. Covering her mouth with both hands, she screamed in front of the crowd, "Like. Oh, my Gawd. Like, you guys are wearing the same shoes! Like. Look, everyone. Oh, my Gawd!"

Everybody's eyes dropped to the floor, and sure enough, both I and "the bitch" were wearing the same black shiny shoes from Payless Shoe Source. A thick gold chain across the top was supposed to resemble couture Chanel, but they were really cheap knock-offs. My arch enemy and I immediately stopped our tirade, hot-faced and embarrassed. I was glad, too. That meant I didn't have to pull her hair or something.

The thought of the past makes me laugh now. We should never take life so seriously. The good has definitely outweighed the bad. Life is meant to be enjoyed, savored. We're supposed to be having fun! The Spiritual Sacred Energy Life Force (Spiritual SELF) always manages to laugh at life, regardless of how cuckoo it can get.

I watch my sister merge into the crowd, still clasping the beer bottle, and I wonder if she's going to slam it into the gal or use her fist. Suddenly, from out of the blue, two identical strangers snatch my sister's balled hand. One handsome man offers her a cigarette, the other one lights it, and then they lead her in the opposite direction for a dance. Within seconds my sister's mood has shifted dramatically, and I watch her sip beer with a satisfied grin and grind to another Black Eyed Peas song. "Everybody! Everybody! Let's get into it! Get stupid! Get retarded! Lose Control!"

Seoul Siblings

*The real miracle is not to walk either on water
or in thin air but to walk on earth.*
—Thich Nhat Hanh

Back at the hotel, I'm hyper-vigilant. I've never been so curious. If I hear anyone say the word "agency" or "searching for birth parents," I'm listening. I'm listening to conversations from behind me, in front of me, across from me—across the room! I'm even searching the Internet for stories. I'm trying to stop but have become obsessed. *Ugh.* I'm driving myself crazy! When I pore over private adoptee message boards, my heart sinks at their muffled voices—stories purposely avoided by glorious adoption agency magazines and advertisements. I can't help but notice that when we smile for the camera, we're given pats on the back and praised. I had no clue there was another side. Hasn't adoption been a win-win for all?

I am sitting with Jenette in the grand ballroom for lunch Sunday around noon. The vast space is dotted with large round banquet tables that each seat at least ten. The stacking chairs are covered with thick white linens and tied in the back by large royal purple bows. White panels and high ceilings make a regal environment. Multiple crystal chandeliers hang from the ceiling. I can't believe I'm here. This vacation has become so thought-provoking, so significant. Sadly, the conference is almost over.

Jenette and I somehow manage to find a seat amongst an all-female group. According to their suit jackets, slacks, and English slang, they must have flown in from the states. They're outspoken, and this particular morning, they're squabbling on the topic of adoptions. Jenette and I sit together at the table, secretly bird watching and pretending to squawk amongst ourselves. We can only pick up crumbs from their conversation. One woman is particularly vocal concerning the adoption experience, even using the word "abductees" to describe us adoptees (what I call "unknown" birds). Despite the fact that she loves her beautiful swan parents, she lives with a hidden sorrow that she has no one but other "unknown" birds—a rare breed to find—to share with. The flock she was raised in picks and pecks at her for squawking and ruffling feathers. "Unknown" birds are supposed to be "grateful" for our capture into "civilization," as instructed, and we're not supposed to mention the losses. As a wee peep, she had been unaware that she had any right to disagree with her stunning swan parents, whose words were law. With no right but to accept her fate, in this new and peculiar pecking order, her "new" and "improved" parents had every right to hit and humiliate her. She felt like she wore a target on her back as they stalked and gawked at her every move.

I nudge Jenette's leg under the table with my heavy black boot. She nods, indicating to me that she's listening. We can't believe these adoptees' stories. Jenette and I have always had each other to talk with. After our own fair share of worms, we tended to forget the favoritism our striking swan mother couldn't help but give to her natural-born swan son (who could do no wrong), flushing negative thoughts into our subconscious. We just assumed we had no right to complain since we were adopted. But, when listening to these rare birds, the worms seem to slip out from the can, and our past comes alive. It's obvious these women can't help but love their adoptive families—perfections and imperfections included—but that doesn't mean they should forget their core self and all it's related to.

Jenette and I have been fortunate to be adopted together. We have a bond that is typical of many twins. We are so close, it would be impossible to tear us apart. We've been through everything together. We often claim that we managed to survive our dazzling parents' troubled marriage and the life they gave us because of our biological bond. Their marriage looked great from the outside, and most people, if they were to judge on appearances, agreed our adoptive parents were happy, even superior. But much of the time, the air inside the house drizzled with dysfunction, depression, and despair.

Mom was what is called these days as a "hoarder." She packed the four-thousand-square-foot house with store-bought treasures (what we, kids, called junk). The boxes of things were meant to save the family from another "Depression," instead, they *caused* a depression. To get away from the family disorder, Dad stayed occupied with his own "toys," owning thirteen cars, most not working and in constant need of repair. If Dad wasn't at work, he was fiddling under one of his beloved old vehicles instead of giving his marriage the attention it deserved. I've always thought we were a pretty average family back then. Typical kids, we focused on our parents' efforts and looked past the flaws...

...Although there were challenges, my twin and I don't regret our childhood, similar to many people adopted: we don't complain. We go with the flow. Trying to transform any anger into useful energy. In other words, be angry enough to make a difference if need be, but not so angry that it consumes me, damaging my immune system and emotional well-being. I've placed blind faith in adoptive parents. I hope most see beyond the physicality of the child and are aware of the sacred energy life force within life itself. Therefore these well-to-do parents won't feel the egoic need to play superficial roles, such as "authority figures" or "ownership" over the children.

My childhood challenges don't bother me compared to the way we were used as pawns for *religious* reasons and then forced to abide by the authority surrounding us. I remember how Mom *used* Jenette and me when we were young to fundraise for the church. As child minorities, we made a bigger impact, and therefore, bigger donations came out of our pockets. She dressed Jenette and me down as beggars to raise money for another "child-help" organization. In Dad's ratty old work clothes, we got to limp and crawl up the church aisle and then hand a plea (to help "orphans") to the pastor during one of the church services. The goal was to save third-world children from hell. The congregation commended Mom and Dad for their super morals, values, hard work, and, of course, for their decision to adopt. Sundays were a great esteem builder for our much-loved parents, and I can see how it would be easy to fall victim to the idea of being crowned with glory for adopting, but as much as I thought this upbringing was admirable when a child, now that I am a loving mother who advocates freedom *from* organized religion, I would never wish this rigid training for any child, born in the West or East. I see the value, morality, and the graceful power within humanity.

In the glamorous hotel ballroom, adoptees discuss concerns posted online that reveal how adoptive families sometimes used racist names to describe them. It was impossible to argue with beautiful swan parents about demeaning attitudes and stereotypical comments. In many swan families, I assume, parents try to be sensitive to race issues, but that doesn't mean extended family or the entire flock on the block—not so accepting—does not pick at the "unknown" bird's foreign feathers and features or just make inadvertent but typical racist comments. As a result, one adoptee wrote that she felt responsible for the fowl names. Then, to add to her ordeal, she felt as if other flocks saw her with her flaunting swan parents and hated her for "hanging out with the enemy (and liking it)." Because she had been isolated from other ethnic groups, she "maintained complete silence about issues of racism" and was forced to internalize the "racist bullshit," including feeling guilt for upsetting her parents with her own can of worms.

I whisper into Jenette's ear, "Can you believe this?" I squeeze her wrist under the table, signaling for her to take notice of these outrageous and suppressed opinions. "How sad!"

She nods, and we face each other, pretending to be engaged in our own warble while we pick at our lunch. One thing I know for sure, the mocking of our Asian heritage is easier to tolerate when we can vent to families who can identify with and affirm our frustration instead of brushing discrimination off as if it's no big deal to parents who don't care or even agree with the insults.

Another "unknown" bird confides that fellow species have written online that they have been caged like a "foreign pet, or threat, being introduced into the environment." One female, in particular, hated being "the object of her parents' humanitarian efforts, in what amounted to twisted racist love." Her feelings concerning her dislocation have never mattered; she was supposed to appreciate the entrapment. As long as adopt*ers* appear to be lovebirds to professional birdwatchers, life in the golden and gilded cage is seen as a blessing. Since many adopt*ers* even go as far as to claim that God is on the *adoptive parents'* side, many of us wonder if adoption serves the wanting couples more than the child.

Mom's chronic unjustified accusations against Jenette and me as "sinning" and "selfish" kids simply felt like what we called back then, *Mom's wrath*. We didn't know others out there in adoptionland existed. Now, I wonder if "loving" adoptive parents are an archetype: lead outwardly pleasant and financially stable lives at the time of adopting, but by the time the kids are grown, are so tired of the responsibility, they take the frustration out on the kids, become engulfed with health problems, bankrupt because of mismanagement, but, of course, awarded top honors and an angelic reputation because it's obvious they've "adopted" someone else's kids. The kind of "forever families" the adoption industry likes to flaunt but never acknowledges problems as the years go by. It's fun to have a baby at first, but the same as any commitment, the honeymoon phase can sizzle quite fast. The adoption agencies are long gone when the realities of the situation enter the scene, and it takes more work and love to raise a child than the adopter expects.

Certainly, natural parents are not perfect, and I'm sure lead just as dysfunctional lives, but what gets me (now that I know the mothers in the East have been counseled out of their parental rights) is the fact that agencies paint wanting couples as saints and the Korean parents as sinners, not recognizing that everything changes: one day the adopting couple might be wealthy and saintly but ten years down the line they might be poor and sinners. One day the Korean parents might be poor and sinners, but ten years down the line, they could be generous and saintly. The agency shouldn't be able to play God and grant certain people other people's kids based on that person's status at the moment and a check for payment. Everything changes. Life changes.

The women's comments are hard to hear, even for us. These are generally issues we didn't discuss for the probability of being misconstrued for ungratefulness by professional bird catchers and even by our closest friends and family. Lots of "unknown" birds have been sent to swans who actually know how to bond and how to give appropriate nurturing and protection (instead of adopting to fulfill a dogmatic conscience). Despite this, there are many rare birds unable to share their can of worms—a can that kicks the happily-ever-after fairytale out the window. There's so much adoptive parent chitchat about that have to do with rescue, saviorhood, and the sacrifices they make for "adopting," yet it's the adopted children who are making the most breathtaking and life-changing sacrifices of all. Voices that have the audacity to speak truth to power have been ignored by the wolves guarding the henhouses.

The women sit next to us, not really minding if we listen since we're adoptees too. Then they flutter away for the next group discussion as if their chirps are no big deal. I guess adoption isn't all castles in the sky. Fortunately, the spirit is exceptionally durable. We're able to deflect the sticks and stones (and even the words) that have been unintentionally (or even intentionally) hurdled our way. Many flocks sing, "What doesn't kill us makes us stronger" (sometimes ducking helps)—this is true for unknown birds. Whether we've been sent to lovebirds or cuckoo birds, we, somehow, manage to shuffle through (on a scorching hot cement path or an ice-cold one) and focus on the bright blue skies more than the lowdown smut and muck. Trust and faith in our Sacred Energy Life Force (authentic power) and the Great Big Bird help us along the way.

i am waiting, Longlong time

The Four Buddhist Noble Truths:
1. Suffering exists.
2. There is a cause of suffering.
3. Suffering can be stopped.
4. The Path to our True Nature.

After the final speeches, remarks of gratitude, and good luck from conference organizers, everyone disperses from the conference ballroom. The anticipation of meeting Korean families for the first time or reuniting with separated siblings charges the atmosphere with the thrill of the unknown. Everyone is table-talking over something. Meanwhile, I have another item on my agenda before we leave. Throughout the conference, I've been nervously caressing the envelope from the Korean man who stopped me in the back alley. I finally found out who's name is written on the front by looking it up in the directory. Turns out, she's a Holt official—one of the first to be adopted and considered an expert in the field. It appears as if the Koreans particularly respect her because she's Amerasian and authoritative in appearance. The agency probably hired her because she's able to effectively promote adoption due to her status as an adoptee.

She wears a bright Western two-piece suit, and her hair flows down her back.

I wait for the official to finish talking with individuals before approaching her. "Ma'am?" The woman's full name is written on a piece of paper given to me by the mysterious man. "Ma'am?"

"Yes?" Without knowing who I am, the older Korean-born Amerasian adoptee reaches out with a welcoming hand.

"May I talk with you?" I ask while other adoptees scout last-minute acquaintances for final photos, thank-yous, and good-byes. It's already Sunday, the last day of the Gathering. The Closing Ceremony has just ended, and expectations for the future have been discussed. Tomorrow, Jenette and I will be leaving for a tour of the country led by a male adoptee.

"Yes." With a tender tug, she pulls me by her side.

"I need to tell you, a man approached me when I was in the back alley behind the hotel."

"What?" She gasps.

"I was at the bottom of the alley coming out of an Internet Café when I saw him at the top of the cement drive. I didn't know what he wanted. At first, I thought he was some sort of protester. When I got closer, I wondered if he was going to attack or something. He kept staring at me. I turned around to see if there was anyone behind me, but I was the only one in the alley. When I realized no one would see if he tried to kidnap me, I got even more scared. So I started looking for escape routes. I thought I was a pretty fast runner, so I could probably run back down the alley if . . . ."

"Oh my! What did he do?" She struggles to breathe.

I slide the envelope out of my front pants pocket. "He gave me this."

"What is it?"

"I don't know, but it has your name on it."

"What does it say?"

"I don't know. I was too afraid to open it."

"Did he say anything when he gave it to you?"

"No. Just a bunch of stuff in Korean. He didn't speak English. So it was really hard to communicate, to understand."

Inside the envelope is a thick, tight triangle made from a flimsy sheet of paper. It had been folded the way an officer folds the American flag when presenting it to a grieving widow at the funeral.

Hesitant, the executive carefully loosens the tucked-in flap of the triangle and unwraps the paper. She offers me a peek. The tiny lettering is crooked, almost childlike, but I sense that each word has been meticulously thought out:

> I want study English !! because, i want talking with my son. He is addaping(?) 2003☐form seoul, to U.S.A.. I am waiting ... for meet, longlong time !
>
> help me please
>
> 2004.08.

Both of us are shocked; however, we're also relieved. At least it wasn't a bomb threat of some sort like I had feared.

"Thank you," she says. "I will take care of this."

Oh, my gosh. I stand in disbelief. My heart opens in the middle of the grand ballroom. How many other Korean parents are looking, and how many are actually getting through to the only people they think will help? Are resources available for birth parents to connect with us? This searching father has no idea who he's up against. Western society dismisses him as an inadequate father. No one acknowledges Western discrimination against Asian men. They're often depicted by ridiculous stereotypes, and society seems to believe these notions as if they're total truth—as if there is nothing more to who these men are. Since these depictions are the only ones shown on television, even I fell for some of the images—that is, before I met my husband during the years before being exposed to people of my ethnicity. Before this trip, I hadn't thought much about Korean fathers. Or that I even had one. Did adoption agencies obtain permission from every Korean father before they expedited us overseas? Or have they managed to legally avoid this?

At first, I wander around the grand ballroom in meaningless circles, feeling lost. Coming together during this conference, I've gained insights into this unique culture that I've been shielded from in order to protect me from my Korean parents. *Hmm. Interesting concept. To be protected against my birth parents by outsiders who believe they knew what was better for me.* At this point, I don't know whether to thank them or curse them.

Of course, the first person I think of is my sister. I gotta tell Jenette! Where is she? My walk turns into a jog into the lobby. I bet she's in our hotel room, packing for the tour. *I need to get onto one of those elevators.* Soon, I'm off and running.

My twin charges around the corner, and we almost slam into each other as if raging lunatics. She yanks me close for more gossip. "There you are. I've been looking for you! I've got to tell you something."

I grip her arm, "There you are. I've been looking for you! I've got to tell you something." I, too, yank her close for more gossip.

We snatch an open elevator, thankfully isolated. "Janine. Okay. There are five sets of twins. Three are from the U.S., one set is from Belgium. And, of course, the famous French twins."

"You'll never guess what that note said," I confide.

She pushes the floor elevator button. The thick doors close, and the elevator rises. It's obvious she's on cloud nine. "We've got to get our picture taken with all the twins. Together!"

"It was a father looking for his son. No one ever told us there were fathers looking. It's gonna be hard to find us. Especially due to the language barrier."

"Janine. That reminds me! The French twins found their birth parents. And get this." My twin seizes my shoulders with both hands. "Their parents never intended to give them up for adoption!"

"What? Hmm." I frown, suspecting foul play. When the elevator hits the seventh floor, we rush to our room in an identical sprint.

Jenette's energy level is charged to the max, and she tells me more. "Instead, the birth parents temporarily placed them in an orphanage or what they thought was a foster home with the full intention to get their twins back once they had their finances in order."

I skid to a halt, practically tripping over my sandals. "Oh, my gosh. That's horrible."

"When the parents went back to the orphanage to pick the twins up, they were gone!" Jenette whispers, "Already shipped off to France without any notification."

"Or permission," I dare suggest.

My sister clutches my arms, and I clutch hers. We study each other's eyes and say the same thing at the same time with the same emphasis. "What if that happened to us?"

Two Birds in the Bush

I hear, and I forget. I see, and I remember. I do, and I understand. —Confucius

When Jenette and I take off for the Korean countryside, we get a bird's eye view of the culture and see that the Great Big Bird belongs to the land and love is, also, in the Korean people. What a concept! We could never wing it by ourselves. Nope, we'd be too chicken. The club of fellow "unknown" adoptees makes this flight of passage for us possible. Along the way, we pass houses cuddled in the country foothills, tall buildings boasting Samsung and American corporations, and areas populated by traditional temples and housing. Bungalows are short and rectangular, and they squat incognito in the layers of rice fields. The hills get steeper, and dirt roads climb through fields of green tea. The weather is hot and humid as we flitter from nest to nest. There are no houses painted in bright pastels of springtime joy. Rather, the houses are earth-colored. The residents' ability to be content with who they are, rather than attempting to be super-sized, makes me think they're supernatural. Anyone can obtain happiness when surrounded by materialistic desires, but I believe that it's just as valuable to learn from those who have found joy from earth mother's natural beauty. *I'm earning my wings!*

For three nights and four days, we stay at Gyeongju. One of my favorite places is the Tombs of Shilla, where they say, "the spirit of 2000 years is still alive." The ancient city is the capital of the Shilla Dynasty, which flourished for 992 years. The city is now considered a museum without walls. Buddhism was officially adopted, becoming its philosophy and culture. Talented masons used crafted stones to create monuments with gold, bronze, and iron. In 1995, the United Nations Educational Scientific and Cultural Organization (UNESCO) designated Bulguksa Temple and Seokguram Grotto as prestigious historic sites because of their two-thousand-year-old cultural heritages. Numerous Buddhist statues beautify the city. The Bulguksa Temple, built-in 528 A.D., got its present name "Bulguk," which means hope for the creation of a clean and comfortable country.

Taenungwon (Tumuli Park), located at the edge of downtown Kyongju, is the biggest of all Shilla tomb clusters. From above, the tombs resemble clusters of grassy tumors. The bodies of royalty had been buried with various personal ornaments, daily utensils, weapons, horse fittings, and even a gold crown. A total of 3,000 relics were extricated and placed into Kyongju National Museum. Koreans believe that by understanding the past, society will be better able to eliminate future problems. One cannot help but feel at peace when exploring the sun-touched paths hugging these manicured green knolls.

As Jenette and I dilly-dally around, I ponder the culture we know nothing about, and it makes me feel like a silly goose. Now I know how Eastern birds feel when they migrate to the West. They must feel so uneasy and unsure of themselves—as if they're always watched by all-knowing eagle eyes! Learning how to follow the ways, the rules, and the calls of each bird sanctuary takes time. Flashes of the stupid things I've done cause a snicker to erupt into laughter. It would probably take years to learn how to adapt to this country, to flap my wings the way the Koreans do!

"Oh, my God, Jenette. I feel like a freakin' birdbrain," I admit, following my twin around the paths adjoining the ancient royal tombs. Giant round mounds range from 22 meters high to 82 meters in diameter at the base. The double gourd shape mounds are joint burial tombs, where the Shilla people laid to rest deceased kings and queens.

"Why? What'd you do?" She asks, snapping a picture of one of the perfectly shaped round hills. Then she checks her gigantic black camera, making sure it's still functioning. It's embarrassing to see her with it—especially compared to everyone else's tiny silver digital ones. Her camera resembles an odd tape recorder from the nineteen eighties that should have been tossed to the birds long ago, and she's not embarrassed to flaunt and flutter it around. When we visited Samsung, she plunked the big plastic camera through the security conveyor belt. The thing was so huge the guards studied it as if it was a massive American toy.

If I could speak Korean, I'd joke, "Yes, you really can take pictures with the thing." Every time I hear it zoom in and out of focus, my face gets warm. I can't help but to think how we're in South Korea—one of the electronic capitals of the world—and Jenette and I are the last to catch up with their advanced technology. (She doesn't know I have a Wal-Mart disposable in my bag.) Unfortunately, because we're identical twins, we can never pretend we're not related.

"I feel like the biggest idiot on the entire planet," I admit again while we wander the ancient tombs.

"Why? What'd you do?"

"I inadvertently told the guide's wife to 'come here' with my palm up." I wince at the shameful thought. "I hope she wasn't offended!"

A husband and wife team has dedicated much of their lives to adoptees. They lead us on this tour throughout our motherland and guide us throughout the exploration into historical regions of the country—sites that we would have been too timid to try on our own due to the language and cultural barrier.

"So, you waved to Mrs. Kim with your palm up," Jenette says, not yet grasping the insult. "Big deal."

"It is a big deal! That's only done to dogs. To people, we're supposed to wave at them to 'come here' with palm down. I didn't mean to wave at her the wrong way!"

"So, Koreans wave like this?" Jenette sticks the hideous camera under her arm, then shows me a waving motion with her palm facing the brick path.

"Yeah."

"And not like this?" She waves with her palm up like everyone does in the states. "Why?"

"The Koreans wave that way to tell *dogs* to 'come here.'"

"Wow." My sister grabs her camera again. It's so big she uses both hands to grip it. "That's different."

"The tour guide told us this before the trip. Remember?"

My sister thinks for a moment before replying. "He did? Why don't I remember?"

"At the briefing, before we left for the tour. We were in a gigantic circle." I reminded her.

"I must not have been there."

"Yeah, you were." I push her slightly. "You were perched across from me."

"I was?"

"Yeah."

"I really don't remember that."

"I remember you were there. You were roosted across from me, and you were staring at him like a hawk the entire time as if you were paying attention to everything he was saying."

"How do you know?"

"Cuz, I was watching you."

"You were watching me?" She holds the camera up to her face and snaps another photo of one of the tombs. The black camera is so large, it practically covers her entire face. She pushes the button, and as if a small engine, the instrument comes alive with chirrups as if it's got the hiccups.

"Yeah. I was watching you. I saw you stare at the tour guide."

"That's weird. Why did you have your eyes on me?"

"I just noticed you were staring at him, but I knew you weren't paying attention."

"How do you know?"

"I just know."

"Whatever. That's just weird." She adjusts the camera for the next shot and then sticks it under her arm again. "So, the Koreans wave this way?" She wiggles her hand with her palm down.

"Yeah."

After a moment of silence, Jenette breaks into a laugh. "Oh, my gosh. I've been waving the wrong way to people during the entire trip!"

I roll my eyes, and we wander through another set of larger-than-life royal graves. Temples and tombs serve as gateways to the past, tangible monuments built thousands of years ago. "So, you didn't do anything stupid during this trip?" I ask, sure that she'll at least think of something, miffed that she agreed with me, hoping that I'm not the only cock-eyed dumb cluck.

She pauses a long while, then hoists the ridiculous camera up to her face to snap another photo with both hands. The flash goes off, and we're in broad daylight. After that, she drops it in her bag.

"Come on," I press, "Haven't you done *anything* stupid?"

My twin shrugs. "Nope. I don't think so. I can't think of anything." And so we continue on our journey into the unknown, like two birds in the bush.

The Missing Link

Everything has its beauty, but not everyone sees it.
—Confucius

We're in Jeju City, located on the central north shore of Jeju-Do Island at the tip of Korea's peninsula. After spending close to a week with the gang—my newly found "culture club" I get the opportunity to listen to more motivating stories. During the day, we visit the waterfalls off the edge of subterranean cliffs and visit the beach and amusement park. At night we break into smaller groups to roam the boardwalk close to the hotel, looking for food and entertainment so we can start our discussions again. Controversial topics dominate our conversations: politics, religion, corporate takeovers, relationships, society's ills and achievements, and finally, adoption. These are hot topics, and discussing them can ignite the fire within. We hold a variety of beliefs, and because we're connected by a common identity and circumstance, we can end the discussion before finishing and continue onward to the next topic, agreeing to disagree.

I've heard rumors that once our Korean mothers are found, they tend to be overbearing compared to what we're used to—at least compared to our Western parents. Asian parents try to fulfill their children's every desire with meticulously selected food, gifts, and attention. For someone who grew up without such attentiveness, the Korean mother's undivided attention can feel a little too close for comfort. I can identify with the problem of trying to balance my motherland and my fatherland—both steeped in morals and values. It was tricky for me to adapt to being surrounded by my in-laws, recent immigrants, who seem to never tire and are incessantly giving to me. I've discovered Eastern mothers find it gratifying to use food as a tool to give affection to their loved ones. According to what I've read from actress Doris Roberts (the famous smothering mother from Everybody Loves Raymond) book, *Are You Hungry, Dear? Life, Laughs, and Lasagna*, Italian mothers have the same reputation of smothering their young. More than a few adoptees find it awkward to acclimatize to smothering doting and become frustrated at their newfound mother's insistence for them to eat. The Eastern mother might interpret the chronic no from their children as a refusal of love. Once the reunion occurs and the honeymoon stage is over, there's a clashing of cultures, preventing a potential bond to transpire. The language barrier is a major problem, and it adds to the unending division.

One of our destinations is Hallim Park, located west of Mt. Hallasan and along the beach of Hallimeup. A tourist brochure boasts that the park faces Biyangdo Island, Hyeopjae Beach, and Geumneung Beach. We have the choice of climbing cliffs, playing on the beaches, or visiting Hallim Park. Jenette and I choose the park. In the early 1970s, a forty-year-old man named Bong-Gyu Song began designing and cultivating the area. He loved Jeju Island so much, he dreamed of a world-class recreational park to attract tourists. By the time our tour group arrives, the location has evolved into a lush land that looks as if it's been around for a million years. Over two thousand varieties of exotic plant life had been seeded in the gardens, including flowers, fruit trees, palms, and cacti. Lava rocks, ponds with lotus blooms, fish, and statues dress much of the area. The most popular tourist attractions are the Hyeopjaegul and Ssangyonggul

"Double Dragon" Caves, known to be the only two-dimensional caves (a cave within a cave) in the world.

With the camera in hand, Jenette and I scour the ancient replica of the "Jurassic-park"-setting. The park is blessed with many areas of interest. I instantly fall in love with the tropical paradise—indeed, a natural wonder. Traditional thatched houses in the Jae Am Folk Village replicate how Koreans lived in the past. The straw roofs were tied down to prevent them from being blown off during typhoons. The walls and foundation are made of stone. Kimchee jars, in multiple sizes, dominate one side of the property. Specific gardens and outdoor resort features make me feel right at home. Hundreds of potted bonsai trees, some barren, some tiny, some lush, some blossoming, some as old as 500 years, decorate the Jeju Rock Potted Plant Garden.

After Jenette and I visit the Bonsai Garden and the Jae Am Folk Village, we stop near a giant birdcage, which serves as an entrance to the "Garden of Beautiful Birds." I study the map. There are several gardens to choose from: Washingtonia Palms, Foliage Plants, Palm Trees, and Kiwi Fruits.

"Do we really want to see the birds?" I ask my sister, squinting at the tiny drawings, uninterested.

She shrugs, working the camcorder.

I can barely make out the map's tiny drawings and colorful images. I see areas of potential interest: Pine Tree Hill, the Water Garden, or the Cherry Blossom Garden. "Oh, I should bring back photos of the cherry trees!" I say, remembering my husband's ardent comments for the pink blossoms. I render a mental note to add the trees to our agenda.

"Sure. Yeah," my sister agrees. "We can do that next."

Mapping the route, I notice a tiny illustration of black birds. That's when I squawk and flap my wings: "Oh, my God! Yes!"

Jenette's eyes bulge at my sudden antics. "What's wrong with you?"

"Ostriches!" I jump and scream.

"What the heck?" Jenette drops the backpack with the water bottles.

"Ostriches!" It's a minute drawing, barely a quarter of an inch small, but I can still recognize their muscular flightless bodies, sturdy legs, and long necks. *According to the map, we must go forward. No turns. No curves. No roadblocks.* With an excited heart, I run toward my favorite animal. *This could be nirvana.* Jenette follows. She points the camera toward me and zooms in on my mania.

As soon as I arrive at the fenced area, two of the five ostriches prance over. I squeal, "My babies!" Why do I love ostriches? I am attracted to the male mating call. Eyes glued to the female at every moment, he pursues her around a dry desert savannah, letting her know he's interested. Depending on his testosterone level, his neck swells red because of the passion he feels. A "red neck" means he's from the east; "blue necks" are from the south. Following the female ostrich around the African grounds, he hollers, sways, and swoops, calling for her with low mating sounds—a call that is undetected by other animals. Although she flounces away from him, she discreetly exhibits interest by flirtatiously fluffing out her brown wings, showing off rare beauty. The male takes notice and goes into what I call a power dance. He sinks onto hocks and waves massive arms covered by black plumage, back and forth, out and about, dancing an enticing rumba, wrenching his head from side to side. He will, at this time, inflate his neck area and create a loud booming noise to attract attention.

The receptive female is forced to turn around and watch, awestruck at the dramatic dance, swift moves, and his overall attractiveness. Impressed but determined to act indifferent, she saunters away, pretending to ignore his banter. She continues to flirt with her head down, popping her beak and shaking her wings, knowing he will soon approach her for mating.

The harmony of the two reminds me of the symbolism used on the Korean flag: the design representing the principles of yin and yang. The upper red section from the circle in the center of the flag denotes the proactive cosmic forces of the yang, and the lower blue section indicates the responsive cosmic forces of the yin. The two pieces together embody the concepts of continual movement, balance, and harmony that exemplify the realm of eternity. Both sides are needed for the other to exist; neither side is worth more than the other. The thick black lines at each of the four corners symbolize one of the four universal elements: earth, fire, water, and heaven—so similar to early Western science's "earth, fire, water, air."

A black-feathered male ostrich stretches his neck to look at me, then the old soul smiles.

By the time Jenette arrives with the camcorder, I'm offering the attentive male baby talk. "Hi, honey. I am here now. I can see you. I know exactly who you are. I see you."

Sensing my love affair with the bird, my twin watches me for a few minutes before commenting, "You are so weird," she says. Then she shudders. "They're eerie. They're not of this world."

The ostrich opens his beak to speak, and I can read his mind. Oh, how I want to pet him and rest in the fluffy, feathery nest-like plumage. The chain-link fence and bushes keep us separated, though, causing my time with the creature to be bittersweet. Someone needs to take care of the ostriches! I fumble around and eventually pull out a Wal-Mart disposable camera from my handbag, not caring if I resemble a tourist. I adjust the itty-bitty thing and take a few snaps.

My sister laughs and points her finger at me. "Where the heck did you get that puny thing?"

"What thing?"

Jenette points to my hand, holding the object wrapped in paper. "That thing. Is that a camera?"

I ignore her rude comments and snap more pictures.

Fascinating creatures! Once agreeing to become partners, ostriches work together for the sake of the children—the future. During the day, the female will protect the eggs with her body of brown feathers that match the dirt Savannah so the male can scout for food. On returning home in the late evening from a day of hunting, the male ostrich gives the female a wild identity dance—swooping large black feathers back and forth specifically for her so she can discern that, yes, he is her mate and not a stranger. How thoughtful! And I can imagine that the female is happy to see him, and the dance makes her laugh. Then the male takes control of the night shift, wrapping the eggs with his black body, camouflaged against the night sky, so the female can scout the wilderness for food. What beautiful beings! These are the native yin and yang creatures, working together for the triumph of the entire family.

Both the male and the female ostrich intrinsically know that they both have distinct instincts aiding survival and that these supernatural powers (one to nourish, the other to protect) are no less or more valuable. Their innate abilities are unique but important, both sacred. Also, both know that one has the capacity to perform the duties of the other, and the physical body might help or hinder the tasks at hand. As the babies grow, the family stays close, ready to react to danger, willing to protect members from being targeted and taken by bird hunters. I suspect that it is because of this teamwork that ostriches have survived for two million years. A prehistoric animal, but oh so advanced! The only feature that can cause folks to become uneasy around these animals is their humongous eyes that seem to see right through a person. *Hmm. Better be on our best behavior!*

After observing me, Jenette whines, "Why do you love ostriches, anyway. They're kinda, um, how should I say it?" She hesitates, and her body tightens. "Weird looking."

Clicking my plastic camera, I brush away her remarks, intent on 'staying in the now.'

"The way they look at me gives me the creeps. Something about those eyes." My twin nitpicks and nags. "Like they're from outer space or something."

"They're evolved," I reply, taken by their primitive yet advanced community.

Jenette grabs my shoulders from behind and directs me away from the fence. "Enough, already," she lectures. "Come on. Let's get something to drink."

I wave bye-bye as if they're humans, hoping that one day I'll be able to love and care for the ostriches the way they should be loved. We enter a store outside of the birdcage for something cold and to find respite from the humid heat. We plunk down on a wooden bench to wait for our order, when . . . .

Oh, my gosh! The curious face of Mr. Ostrich appears through the window! I giggle and wave.

"Oh great," Jenette says, sighing. "Fine, you win. Let me take pictures of you and your big dorky birds."

I hand her my camera, and she inadvertently flings it up in the air. "Wow! This thing is light as a feather! It's tiny compared to my camera. Are you sure it actually takes pictures?"

"Umm. Get yours out too. Just in case."

Jenette juggles both cameras: her enormous black one, my minuscule white one. After the photoshoot, the ostrich and I have this weird staring contest. When I'm the first to blink, the creature flirts by, perusing the grounds in prance and spreading out its feathers. My twin rolls her eyes and quivers in disgust at my obsession.

My God! It's as if we've known each other for millions of years. Why do I love ostriches? The energy of these creatures reminds me of primitive cultures, such as the Aborigines in Australia. Some aborigine tribes have been in existence for 50,000 years! To be a member of one of these magnificent tribes fascinates me! They passed long-distance messages to each other by way of energy. They could read each other so well, they barely needed to communicate verbally as "civilized" societies do. The conversation was at a minimum and even telepathically. Unfortunately, same as Eastern philosophers and intuitive women, tribes have been presented as being the "most primitive, wretched people on the face of the earth."[17] by those who couldn't grasp the unseen treasure. I don't believe the indigenous tribes were inferior in any way, shape, or form—they just appeared to be a threat against the foreign man who couldn't *see* the value or the essence of the tribes; therefore, they were not so allowing of their existence.

My twin taps my shoulder. "Umm, Janine. Umm. It's time to go," she lectures, stirring me out of my foolish imagination. "Get your head out of the ground."

"Shh." I wave her away. I need time with my family. At this moment, I belong to the ostrich family—the missing link!

"Umm, Janine." She tugs on my arm. "It's time to go!"

"But ostriches! We've found our family!" I am the ugly duckling who belongs to the ostrich family. I admit, they're not the most beautiful or graceful bird on planet earth, and, no, they can't fly, but they have a bounce in their step, and their feathers are fluffy and magical.

"Umm, Janine." My twin drags me out of the café and shudders. "You need help. You really do belong to a funny farm."

Love for the creatures—my little family, my long-lost family, fills me with family bliss. Strange? A little. Peculiar? Yeah. Able to fly? No. Spirited? Of course. The missing link? You be the judge. *Time really does fly when you're having fun!*

Freedom Day

*"For transcultural adoptees, our lives are written in pencil.
Everything you think you know about yourself
can change in an instant."*
—Bryan Thao Worra, Laotian Adoptee, and Poet

On the hour-long plane ride from Jeju-Do Island back to Seoul, my mind drifts. I mull over the possibility of meeting my Korean mother at the Sofitel hotel. It would be nice to at least take a look at her before I go home to the states. I really don't need a long-term relationship, I'd be happy with a mere one-nighter, and then I'm good to go. I'm still holding on to a wing and a prayer that Omma has possibly seen our photo in the newspaper articles and contacted the adoption agency, which in turn contacted someone who tells her we'll be back at the Sofitel this afternoon—after all, it's Freedom Day. How appropriate the reunion would be. Spacing in and out, I partially meditate and then fixate on the sun's glare from the window. Looking down at puffy white clouds, Omma contacts me by the soul, and I'm not sure if this dialogue is real or my imagination or if it matters which:

Janine. I am here. I am here.
Who? Who are you?

Your mother.
What mother?
Your birth mother.
I don't believe it. I don't believe you.
I have died. I have passed on. And now I want to pass onto you—me.
I don't believe it. I need to see you. I don't believe you.
I am here. I am the air you breathe.
I don't believe it. I need to see you. I don't believe you.
I am the plant you seed.
How so? Do not understand.
In the beginning, there was you and me.
How so?
We became one at birth. I am in you. You are in me. We are one. We are the family tree.
How can that be? When we're two separate beings?
You imagine us as separate, but we are not. I have always been with you. In all you do, I've been with you in mind, in spirit. And I always will.
I need proof. This is simply not enough. It doesn't satisfy my soul—my calling. I need to see you. I need to see your physical presence. Where's the proof? Where's the proof?
I am here. I am here. I am near. I am near.
Still, you have no proof.
Look in the mirror. You will see my self. You will see thy self.
How is that proof? I only see me.
You may only see me, but there's so much more than "me," there's "you" and "thee." There's the family tree all wrapped up in one entity.
Still, don't believe. Still, don't understand. I've been without you my entire life.
Open your eyes. Come out of the disguise. Always, I've been with you. I've believed in you. We've lived in harmony, harmony.
You're a stranger to me. Why would I want you here when I don't know you?
You have me whether you want me; whether you know me. You and I are one. We'll always be one whether you acknowledge my presence or you ignore my presence. We will always be one. You live in me; I live in you. We are one. We are one.

Where does that put my adoptive mom?
I gave her temporary custody of you.
What does that mean?
It means she had you for a while. She raised you. She did the work. She made the effort. She manifested her reality. She provided you with a house. But your home will always be with me.
I still don't believe you. I can't see the proof.
There's no need for proof or your belief. What is, is. Truth is truth. Biology is biology. Harmony is harmony. A tree is a tree. Family is family. Melody is melody. Destiny is destiny.
I am waiting for something magnificent to happen.
Life is magnificent. Can't you see how magnificent life is?
I guess I'm expecting a miracle or something.
Just live for today. Live the miracle today. Okay?

The tour bus exhales, then heaves to a stop in front of the hotel in the early afternoon on the bright weekend. Multiple adoptees, at various ages and stages of the family search, step onto the sidewalk. Many, I've learned, don't feel the need to look; others have already experienced live reunions and used the trip to visit with blood families.

The women wait for the driver and his helpers to pull out luggage from the bus's belly. I scan the street for people who resemble me. Shiny black cars fly by on the gray pavement. *Nope. Not yet.* My focus is glued to the hotel entrance. They must be inside, waiting for us. Jenette and I, along with our friends, wheel our bags through the open doors and scuttle inside.

That's when I spot a grandfatherly type man standing on the far end of the sidewalk. He's got a poster board sign next to him, with words on the front and back. Could he be a homeless man begging for money with a cardboard sign, similar to those seen on street corners in my hometown? Or could he be related to me in some way? I point him out to my adoptee friends as we enter the building.

"Who is he?" I ask.

One of them turns around and briefly looks. "Oh, he's probably a Korean against adoption."

I'm amazed at the thought. *There are "real" Koreans against adoption?*

After the bright Seoul sun, the lobby is as dark as a cave. I look for a woman around the age of fifty or a few hidden younger siblings with cameras ready to jump out from behind the doors and yell "Surprise!" (Or, however, it is said in Korean). The shiny marble floor picks up a glimmer of street shine and shimmers in the darkness like an illusion. Shadows are what I see until my eyes adjust.

There's a young Korean couple at the café sipping French coffee, a few families at the reception counter with backs turned toward me and, beyond them, hotel staff thoroughly groomed, collars and suit jackets buttoned, leather loafers polished, talking into telephones. Scanning the lobby, I see no one searching for us. No one looks lost. Nothing out of the ordinary is vying for my attention.

English-speaking Koreans are scattered throughout the lobby in the business office and at the currency exchange counter. It feels identical to a Seattle hotel rather than one in Seoul, a city where I can't communicate, let alone ask simple questions, such as: "Where's the bathroom?" and "How much?" and "Where's Omma?"

Traditional Korean (Han guel) characters on signs and brochures still puzzle me. Thank God for the English translations. Exhausted, Jenette and I park our baggage and ourselves on a red sofa near the middle of the lobby. The air is fragrant with failed hope for a few and success for others—each of us is a little different than we were before.

A female adoptee approaches the couch with a grin. "You won't believe this," she tells us.

"What?" Jenette and I sit up.

"I found my birth mother."

"How?"

"Just by going to the orphanage."

"The orphanage?"

"Yeah. The orphanage. Word was spread about my visit, a quick telephone call, and the next thing you know, there she is."

"Wow!" Jenette and I stare at each other. My twin maintains a conversation. "Did you get the meeting on the camcorder? Did you get photos? Do you look like her? Do you have siblings?"

Meanwhile, I unzip the black bag that holds our documents and bustle through multiple white pieces of paper, concerned that we only have a few hours to visit the orphanage before we must leave this hotel.

The grinning woman's happiness is contagious. It gives us last-minute optimism before we go home. "Visit the orphanage, you guys," she tells us.

"I've found something!" I shove a piece of paper in front of Jenette's face. "CBH. What does CBH mean?"

I immediately think of Mr. Jae, the hotel employee who spoke English, who was always available during the conference to help. He gave a group of us a ride to Itaewon and made photo business cards for Jenette and me with the message, "Please help us find our mother. We were born in June 1972," with our contact information.

"Where's Mr. Jae?"

I turn around and run toward the business office, nestled in a glass case alongside the bellhop counter. Mr. Jae considered more a friend now because of his humanity, sits behind the office desk. At my rushed arrival, he stands and bows. When I'm inside the glass office, the door closes on its own, giving my yelps for attention privacy.

"Mr. Jae. Please help me," I say, with only a few hours left before we need to leave the hotel for the plane ride back to the U.S. "I need to make a phone call, but I don't know how."

The impeccably groomed hotel manager flips open his cell phone and hands it to me with two hands. "You can use mine."

I look at his tiny silver box, then at the crinkled hotel note from a week back with the newspaper reporter's phone number, then back to his tiny silver box. I realize I never got the journalist's name. And I still haven't learned how to make a phone call.

Hesitating, I return the tiny silver cell phone.

"What's wrong?"

"I just found out that an adoptee found her birth mother. Jenette and I need to go to the orphanage. We should never have gone to Holt. We need to go to the orphanage! We should have gone there on the day of our arrival. We need to visit CBH! We're flying out in the afternoon." I point to the crinkled hotel note. "Will you call this reporter?"

"Ah. Yes." He nods, taking the paper from me. "I'll dial the number."

After a few rings, the man on the other end answers. They exchange words, and then Mr. Jae hands the phone to me.

I grab the phone and scream, "Holt won't give adoptees their birth records!" I state without saying hello, or even calling the reporter by his name. I holler into the teeny thing, "You need to write an article about it now!"

No response.

"It's our last day in Korea!"

Still, no response.

"And it might be the last chance that we will find our birth mother!"

"But it is Freedom Day," the reporter finally admits.

Ignorant that Freedom Day is a national holiday celebrating independence from Japan's occupation (similar to the United States' Independence Day), I fall silent to his excuse.

He whispers, "I can't take you to the orphanage . . . . My schedule is full," he tells me. "And I already have plans . . . with my . . ." His voice goes to barely audible "family."

"Then you must write an article," I holler. "You must tell the Koreans that Holt won't give complete and accurate birth information to adoptees. And I'm not even sure if they're giving the truth out to the birth parents. You must tell the Koreans what's going on."

"But, the editor already knows this."

"He does?"

"In fact . . . everyone knows this."

"They do?"

"Yes. I'm sorry, but the editor won't let me do another story on it. The story's already been done. I'm sorry, Jennee."

"Oh. But why?" Scratching my temple, I murmur, "Why was nothing ever done? Why has nothing changed?"

"I'm sorry, Jennee. There's nothing I can do."

And the itty bitty silver phone vanishes from sight.

The Emperor Has No Clothes!

*Any transition serious enough to alter your definition of self
will require not just small adjustments in your way
of living and thinking but a full-on metamorphosis.*
—Martha Beck, O Magazine,
Growing Wings, January 2004

Lots of reunion stories are being passed around. A handful of adoptees have found their relatives by way of the media—at least to my knowledge. I haven't heard many stories of adoption agencies being helpful and readily giving out accurate birth records. In fact, I've only heard just the opposite—but I hope this is wrong.

Before leaving for our Fatherlands—the land we've been raised in—leftover adoptees, now good friends, recline in the lobby, wishing each other well, as one by one, individuals fly back to the West. I've befriended another adoptee who reminds me a lot of myself. We're both in our thirties, only she's a few inches taller than I am and exudes more confidence.

On seeing my friend at the bellhop counter, I wave and smile to get her attention. She has just returned from visiting the same social worker in the same office that Jenette and I had inquired at when we first arrived in Seoul. Since there was little information given out to the adoptees at the Holt booth during the conference, she decided to visit the office in hopes that her information would be there.

"Hey, Kim!" I call out and head her way. "Did that social worker from Holt ever follow through on that appointment you had with her? Did you get to see her at the office?"

"No." Kim pushes her sunglasses up and rests them on the top of shiny black hair. A ponytail is pulled back firmly, keeping loose strands off her face. To me, she looks to be the all-American gal.

"The social worker was there, but in a meeting. She barely acknowledged me when she came in and out of the office. She practically acted as if I wasn't there! And she knew I was coming."

"What? That's too bad. And you requested the information to be there when we got back from the tour. I would think a week or more gave them enough time to pull up your request."

"This has been so frustrating." Kim sighs and drops her bags at the counter. "When I got to the office, her assistant *did* give me some information, but only on the woman who temporarily cared for me."

"Your foster mother? And not your Korean mother?"

"Yeah. Just info on my foster mother."

"Hmm." *I wonder if caseworkers give us descriptions of foster parents to deter the attention from our biological families.*

"I explained that my foster mother also had an eighteen-year-old daughter who helped to care for me, and I requested her contact information. But the social worker stated they couldn't reach her family, and nothing else happened."

"What about your birth records?"

"She told me my records weren't there. They've been sent to Oregon. The only document that was on file was stuff about my foster mother."

"I wonder if the social worker was actually in a meeting or purposely avoiding you."

"I didn't feel welcomed there," Kim says, sighing. "I waited in the chair and never did get the chance to speak to the social worker. She's a disservice to the adoptee community."

I nod and fold my arms.

"Her assistant went back to her two or three times to get answers to questions I had. It's hard for me to believe that the only thing in my file in Seoul is stuff on my foster family . . . And the recent correspondence between the social worker and me that started earlier this year."

Perplexed at what appears to be a cover-up, I offer my own theory: "What gets me is that the social worker is an adoptee, too. It's as if Holt hired her principally to gain adoptee trust. We assume Holt is on our side because there's an adoptee at the front counter. But in reality, she's probably just following orders from whoever is at the top of the pyramid." I stop and remember the gossip Jenette had told me. There was a rumor that the social worker gave more information to male adoptees, especially if they bribed her with beer. I add a secondary thought meant to be funny. "Or the social worker could just be a bitch."

"Actually, there's been a problem at Holt even before her, too," Kim tells me totally serious. "I've been trying to get my records since December 2002."

"Oh, my gosh!"

"After receiving another adoptee's records initially and then getting the wrong information on my Korean parents, it took me three attempts to get what I think is *my* file."

"Man! It's the adoption agencies who should be ashamed of themselves! Not the Korean mothers!"

Kim leaves the counter, obviously distressed and confused over the situation. I turn around and practically bump into a fellow Seattleite with a crew cut, Mariners baseball cap, and navy nylon backpack. He asks if I've heard the latest on a current adoption lawsuit happening in our hometown. This one involves a woman who, since 1990, organized 800 transactions for wanting couples from Cambodia and earned an estimated nine million dollars.

In between sips of bottled water, he barks at me in the middle of the lobby, oblivious to anyone listening. "You mean you haven't heard of the woman by the name of Galindo who started Seattle International Adoptions? I read about her in a Seattle Times article, and she's also been on 20/20 or Primetime, one of those shows. I heard she charged American couples several thousand dollars for a child but only paid the birth parents as low as fifteen dollars. She also paid recruiters around 300 dollars to find and bring children to the orphanage."

"No way." I close my eyes at the thought and shake my head, unbelievingly. "That's outrageous." But then I think a few thousand dollars charged for a Cambodian child is not as greedy compared to almost $30,000 or more as charged by "ethical" agencies for a Korean baby.

"She also wrote that the children's parents are 'unknown' and investigators suspect that the woman falsified immigration documents to appear as if the children had been abandoned when, in reality, many of them had been coerced from their mothers."

"That's outrageous." I think for a moment. "But the weird thing is, that's exactly what happened to us. It seems as if agencies wrote 'unknown' under our birth parents' names too so they could send us overseas." Knowing that these agencies use God's name to justify their business activities and then get painted as saints for the transaction (so we would be followers of their religion) is what bothers me most. It's unfortunate to think that our parents have been led to believe that they were "sinners" or would receive God's wrath and go to hell had they kept us.

The adoptee fiddles with the bottle, twisting the cap off and on, then throws the bottle around. "Galindo even lied to mothers, saying they'd get photos of their children growing up and that later the child would be back to help the family."

"Geez. How deceiving." I wonder how many Korean parents sent photos of families to the agencies to give to their adopted-out children, expecting the gifts would be given to the children, not realizing their children will be taught that the adoptive parents are their "real" and "only" parents. Do the agencies pass on accurate family stories?

The fellow adoptee from my hometown goes on to tell me that Galindo is the first American convicted of baby trafficking and was sentenced to 18 months for defrauding American couples. Galindo and her sister pled guilty to money laundering, visa fraud, and currency structuring in connection with the adoption operation. Galindo claimed that she suffered from post-traumatic stress syndrome, and then, after the case, adoptive parents say they now suffer from post-traumatic stress syndrome. In the end, Galindo was ordered to pay more than $60,000 in restitution to the American couples.

I have to ask, "But, what about the dislocated children and their Cambodian parents? Did they get restitution?"

The male adoptee practically chokes on a swig of bottled water before spitting, "Of course not!" A disbelieving laugh accompanies coughing spasms, and he wipes his mouth with a sleeve. My heart drops at the thought of Korean families who had been taken advantage of and for those who will be. If adoptees question our placement, we get verbally shot down by industry pioneers who claim we're ungrateful.

Recovered, the male adoptee approaches me again. "The question the judge had to consider was whether Galindo was a saint whose mission was to save Cambodian children, or was she a greedy manipulator who exploited the country's poverty."

"It doesn't matter what her intention was," I counter, "to me, the results are the same. In both cases, the families are still separated. Family ties have been cut. Identities forever altered."

"One of the concerns the judge had was what would happen to the Cambodian children when they travel back to Cambodia in search of their families and agencies would refuse to help."

"I know what will happen." As if the answer is obvious, I point to the Korean-born adoptees scattered along Seoul's hotel lobby. Many are content with life and unaware of any wrongdoing—but still empty-handed. "The same thing that's been happening to us."

"International Adoption will never be stopped." My male friend informs me with a surplus of certainty. "Babies are too hot of a commodity. Especially baby girls. Most applicants, these days, want to adopt overseas, anyway," the male adoptee fills me in casually as if referring to livestock or vegetables. "Because then they don't have to compete with American birth parents who have access to lawyers to get their children back. We've been processed by a charitable, religious organization. They've been making shitloads of money off of trading us over and lookin' like angels while doing so." He smirks at his own comments, flips the bottle of water again, and walks off as if all of this is no big deal.

When going through tough times, Jenette and I have tried to laugh at life and look for the future for refuge. So I shouldn't take my adoption so seriously! I shouldn't make this such a big deal. Try to make fun of it. (And if that doesn't work, just make a pun out of it.) *What are we? Sitting ducks? A mother hen could never compete against a million-dollar petting zoo. We're just backyard chickens to these bigwigs. Boy, are the birth parents here in the East forked and done over easy. Nowadays, adoption isn't due to war or even poverty. The last war was fifty years ago. Any nesting woman is fair game. Birth moms better not count their chicks before they hatch. When all is said and done, birth parents are too busy running around in circles with their heads cut off and scratching out a living. It's not like these families have nest eggs to rely on for a lawyer. On the other side, even if adoptive parents are hard-boiled, the adopted child better be sunny-side-up! No complaints! If we peep, these agencies would probably use us as target practice. They'd probably dig up as much dirt as possible. Call us spoiled rotten. What if they wring our necks for being unhappy larks? Do they give a hoot about what's best for the children? And if so, would they be willing to set caged birds free?*

When I fill my sister in with the latest primetime news, she scratches a forehead temple with an acrylic fingernail and massages her chin, mystified. "This is unbelievable. I thought adoption was all *good*. How do they find such willing people to fall for their services?"

"Look at Mom and Dad," I say flatly. "They fell for it."

"Oh, yeah . . . ." Jenette nods. Her voice drops to a whisper. "That's right. It's kinda sad. It's almost as if the agency took advantage of their bereavement by selling the fairytale of a happy family—by adopting a baby or two. They were more susceptible to agency advertisements after losing their own baby girl." My twin sighs heavily, pulling closer to me on the red lobby couch. "It's so deceptive."

I'm relieved to know that my sister exists, at least. It's true. Thank goodness we have each other. We had no idea that such swindling could happen—let alone, to us, of all people. We've simply believed what we've been taught and assumed our adoption was a blessing. And because adopted people have been scattered the world over, there has been no education or discussion over what should be every human being's birthright: family and lineage. Therefore, there is little need to request justice. Most of us are still in the dark concerning this violation of our most basic human rights. Are the agencies too powerful today to be corrected? *Who knew we'd end up on a wild goose chase?* The issue that needs to be addressed is *Why were non-orphaned children allowed to be labeled "orphaned" in adoption marketing campaigns, websites, and even adoption law?*

When I send a message to a European adoptee on these shocking discoveries, she e-mails back: "Welcome to the club of angry adoptees who want to sue these bastards!"

By the end of the one-week tour around South Korea's landscape, Jenette and I have learned more about our motherland than we had for the past thirty-two years. Concerned, we might never be able to travel to Seoul again. Our suitcases, practically as tall as we are, are crammed full. While we stand in line at the check-in counter, we wonder if we have too much baggage. There's an 'excess baggage' charge for those who are carrying more weight than allowed. It's as if we've been starving for a morsel of truth, and Seoul has served as an enormous buffet, filling our lost ethnic identities with joy and memories.

Despite bulging bags overflowing with Korean trinkets, our bags are checked in without trouble. The perfectly coifed Asiana woman behind the counter enters our data into the computer, tags our luggage, and points Jenette and me through with a nod. We're approved to enter the terminal and back to the United States.

Once Jenette and I find our airplane seats, we grab the latest travel magazines and settle in for the long flight home. Opening up STAR, a gossip magazine, I see famous swan princesses are gaining and losing weight. It's quite common to dish out money for plastic surgery in glitzy Hollywood, setting the standard for the rest of society—now the rest of the world. Swan stars and want-to-be stars fork over big bucks to appear more swan-like. I don't have to look hard to find photos of the filthy rich. I flip through a recent issue of BAZAAR fashion magazine, searching deliberately for an Asian face—someone who resembles me. After digesting the entire thing, I toss the magazine aside. There is absolutely no Asian face on its pages. The magazine truly is "Bizarre." How privileged to be fed the line that claims only one beauty: American beauty.

Instead of reading up on the latest beauty techniques created by and for swans, I focus on my own flock. I feel so fortunate to be able to go home to my husband and two daughters. My Vietnamese-born husband turned U.S. citizen (before I did) has definitely given me a whole new world to enjoy—a Vietnamese community I would have never been privileged to partake in if it weren't for his happy childhood in Viet Nam. The mainstream might see his "third world" neighborhood in the early days and wonder how his family managed. Yet, he has fun childhood memories where he could freely roam the mountains with his many siblings and boat and fish in the front yard sea. He had no idea that he was considered "needy." Just because he came from Vietnam, he *never* considered himself needy, and he is staunch in his position to never take hand-outs. In fact, surrounded by natural beauty and fruit and vegetation all around, he enjoyed his childhood. Being married to this guy, I have gained an admiration for him and other immigrants who contribute unique skills, morals, and values to maintain the United States. I thank the Great Big Bird for helping me make the right decision and follow my true SELF when I was young, even though my parents disapproved. I've found it's best to live by my heart instead of dogmatic rules. I may not have found what I was looking for in Seoul, but I get to fly home to my own small nest.

After hours in flight, reflecting on how fortunate I am, the flight status channel shows that we are approaching American air space, and the lights are turned back on. The Asiana flight attendants fly up and down the aisles. I can't ignore their energy and their community, and I'm looking forward to enjoying the future with my own peeps: my husband and daughters when I get home. Unbeknownst to me at this time, my husband is planning a trip to Vietnam for us. He intends to take me to his home village in the "third world."

I know, now, that I am rooted in a culture much grander than I ever thought existed. Thank the Great Big Bird for bird sanctuaries! Life truly is bizarre.

Child Saviors? Or Savior Complex?

God Save Me From Your Followers
—bumper sticker

Lao Tzu once said that recognizing the cycle of life is enlightenment; ignoring it leads to disaster. Do adoption agencies ignore and dismiss the natural cycle of life? After the trip to South Korea, I contacted one of Harry and Bertha Holt's elderly biological daughters to inquire about my adoption papers. Her initial email told me that all the adoptee records had been kept in Seoul until 1975 when North Korea said they would make Seoul "a lake of fire." Consequently, they sent most of the records to the countries the children were sent to, and only a few medical records were kept in the files in Seoul. Therefore, my record could be given to me from the office at Holt International (located in Oregon) for a $400 fee, of course.

Then, three days later, she told me (without realizing she was contradicting herself) that my sister and my files were at the office in Seoul—the same office Jenette and I had visited. In an email, she wrote that they had purchased land adjoining their Reception Center (now the building includes the Post Adoption Services) and built a Records Storage facility where the adoptee records are currently filed. They were in the process of microfilming them. And they finally succeeded in getting everything into the computer in about 2001.

Ms. Holt's next question to me is a common one—a question I'm sure many adoptees have heard before. She asked, "Have you ever thought of what might have become of you if you hadn't been adopted?"

Yes, for my entire life, I believed I would have died if it wasn't for her organization. I made the assumption that I owed them my life. I placed the agency on a pedestal—something they probably needed and expected from me so that I would donate and/or adopt and keep the adoption spiral going, enlarging their business. She claimed that whoever left us at the street corner wanted us to be found quickly and probably watched from a distance and that, from her experience, twins usually came from families; but sometimes the families weren't prepared for two. This left me wondering: Wouldn't anyone *without an agenda* encourage a scared mother to believe in her capabilities, uplift, and encourage her? And offer resources, or at the very least, invite her into the child care facility? As a young mother who was able to work past my fear and the stigma assigned to me by the church, I know encouragement is the ethical answer when "helping" what they call "mothers in crisis." Ms. Holt's presumptions cause me to think that not even Americans are prepared for two babies, but we don't suggest or counsel the parents to give up their children just because they come as a surprise. In fact, most likely, the parents are bombarded with gifts and help. If they are truly advocates for "family values," agencies should be giving instead of taking away. Even if one parent is missing, other members should be notified before sending a child to a new family.

Ms. Holt also told me that they only take children who have "no functioning" parents to "loving parents" who could give what Holt calls "a *real* life." Her attitude suggests that she presumes my Korean parents to be dysfunctional while routinely assuming evangelical couples were (and still are) more "loving."

As a Korean-American mother, her assumption insults me. All humans from the beginning of humanity have been capable of raising their children even in the most unbearable circumstances. Less severe child protection measures such as temporary care, kinship care, community care, guardianship—and inviting families into the orphanages and hospitals to help with their own child's care could be offered. Changing names and assigning numbers only increase the problem children have when attempting to reunite as adults.

Ms. Holt added that it was hard for some of her staff over the years to understand adoptees coming back to find their roots. "We, Americans knew you would be back and prepared for it as best we could," she claimed, "but Koreans operated the program in Korea for many years now. They are reluctant to tell adoptees things that might be painful for them."

Here, again, Ms. Holt shifts the blame onto the Koreans even though the Koreans she refers to are agencies such as the Holt-Korea, which contributed to Korea's welfare and belief system. I believe Mr. and Mrs. Holt had the best of intentions when they first gained access to children in 1954, yet they have failed to acknowledge every angle of adoption, which should include the missing voices belonging to adopted people and biological families. Now more than fifty years later, the "success" has inflated the egos of the adoptioneers into believing they should be given the monopoly on the world's children. The "child savers" may insist they work for God, but their business activities demonstrate they're benefiting and enlarging their own agenda. In the West, their followers have hailed the evangelicals as saviors, and because of this, they have been allowed to penetrate Eastern government officials, and as a consequence, thousands of families. I'm sure; however, grieving parents of missing children could go as far as calling the organization *sinners*. At least I know a great many transracial adopted people do.

I believe facilitators have a responsibility to tell adopted people the truth even if they speculate that it will be "painful" for us—which is their excuse for keeping information from us. And it is none of their business to know or judge how we handle our reunions if we so choose. Of course, we are aware our blood families will not be perfect, but we also know that our adoptive families came with imperfections. We have a right to handle our business the way we want to. Ms. Holt added, "Also I am sorry to say that many Koreans discriminate against orphans, and thus adoptees unless they are part of a real family," and that Koreans have a "fascination for blood ties" and therefore fought the Holts on their evangelical zeal.

Most Koreans I've come across are curious and saddened when they learn of how the children have been routinely removed. All have been receptive and open-minded to my perspective. No one, yet, has ridiculed or discriminated against my twin and me for our status as adoptees. Many Koreans have not yet, been informed of the life-altering impact international adoption has on the families involved. As for the accusations against Koreans for having a fascination with "blood ties," I know that every civilization should have an interest in blood ties—it truly is a fascinating topic for many of us—especially those who were ousted from ever having contact. I highly doubt that the Koreans are the only ones who care about their offspring and heritage. Every civilization tries, at least, to maintain a historical record of their ancestors and lineage—this is human nature and only referred to as *negative* in adoptive parent circles. Knowing one's roots gives a human strength and a foundation and helps to validate and contribute to who a person is at the moment. Even our Western families have been known for tracking their heritage. We don't accuse them of having an abnormal "fascination" with blood ties.

At last, I was instructed to request our file from a social worker in Oregon, who eventually sent us a partial file. The $400 fee had been waived, and I suspect there's a note stating that I am one of those "angry" adoptees. Actually, I am not an angry (although I do have a right to be) person, but I am angry *at the agency*. I am totally at peace with who I am because I know who I am at the core, which is not the person the agency workers' had thought I was at birth and not the person they think I am as an adult.

The most important message I hope to give to fellow adoptees is that we're all in this together, and, YES, we do belong to something much bigger. We might be misunderstood, rejected, and even demeaned by our loved ones when we speak our truth. Despite this, always remember that when it seems as if everyone else has failed us, keep on keeping on. (My sister's favorite slogan is "keep on going, never stop growing.") Don't ever give up. Don't ever lose sight of who we really are. We are definitely not reduced to who they say we are. We are extremely important, so take care of yourself, especially when it seems like no one else cares. We must care for SELF (Sacred Energy Life Force)! If ever feeling lonely, it's never too late to BE that parent to yourself. Sometimes, we have to be the ones to save ourselves.

The End

ABOUT JANINE VANCE

International multi-award-winning recipient and gold-medalist author Rev. Dr. Janine Vance, Philosophy, has written numerous books in the genres of memoir, anthology, history, politics, and self-help. Vance has been interviewed in newspapers, television, and radio from Seattle, Washington in the United States to Seoul, South Korea, including BBC Radio, Northwest Afternoon, Huffington Post, Northwest Asian Weekly, Dong-A Ilbo, and Chosun.

Visit janinevance.com.

BOOK DOCTOR: A memoir-writing consultant, Janine believes every human has vital experiences to be shared and that history needs to be told by the people most impacted by it. Readers have called her books "great help when things are spiraling," "peaceful," "a gentle reminder," "uplifting," and "highly recommended."

FAVORITE CHARITY: Since 2010, Janine's favorite charity has been Against Child Trafficking (ACT NL). As the director of ACT in the USA, Janine is proud to be on a team rooted in inherent human rights. ACT's first Adoption Trafficking Awareness Symposium brought attention to the adoptee-rights community the crisis of adoption trafficking in 2022. Why has the adoption industry remained in full force locally and worldwide? Society has been led to believe that international adoption is the best option, but there is a hidden side to this practice. It's time to discuss the elephant in the room—how adoption law exploits children into adulthood.

PERSONAL: Between '84 –'21, Janine provided full-time care for her adoptive father, a former aerospace engineer, after a traumatic brain injury from a hang-gliding accident that impacted his speech, balance, and fine and gross motor control skills. Vance's suggestions on coping with trauma can be found in two philosophy books condensed from more than thirty-years of caregiving. Visit vancetwins.com for fun.

A PERSONAL CHILDHOOD STORY
THE ORIGINAL SPECIAL-EDITION VINTAGE-VERSION:

Janine Vance shares how and why her family went from *normal* to *paranormal* in this memoir, the very first book she wrote in her early twenties. *To fellow adoptee-rights activists, please note: this book does not critique adoption but rather shares the author's personal Generation-X coming-of-age childhood experiences.

"I was drawn in right from the beginning, with the descriptions of all the 80's styles and awkward teenage years. It reads like a fiction book with so many interesting details. The descriptions of the family dynamic are given from a very objective viewpoint so the reader really grasps how unfair the situation was without any hint of anger or bitterness in the words. Aside from the adoption community, I really think the spiritual community would be enriched by reading this story. Most of all, I absolutely LOVE the end, when the author talks about her spiritual growth, expanding to other spiritual ideas, and especially how she came to see the deeper meaning in all of those experiences. The last few chapters are so incredibly powerful! By the end, I felt like my spirit was bursting with joy that she came to such a beautiful place of healing and that she generously shared that with others. I Loved it!!!" **AMAZON REVIEWER**

LIGHT-HEARTED PHILOSOPHY FOR ANYONE:

 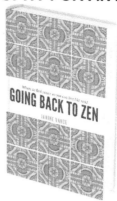

About *The Power of Isolation:* Need to "stay calm and carry on" in today's harsh landscape, which seems so divided on various levels? For anyone of us who has ever been demeaned and demoralized prompted by misconstrued assumptions about who "you" are, use one or two of these ideas for your benefit

"5.0 out of 5 stars An interesting approach to learning how to empower oneself with solitude and alone time. Heavily influenced by Buddhism and Taoism as well as other Eastern philosophy and also by what used to be called New Age spirituality, the author focuses on the benefits and techniques of meditation that one can use to help regulate emotions, become aware of one's inner core, declutter the brain for better decision-making, and empower the S.E.L.F. (Sacred Energy Life Force)."

About *Going Back to Zen:* This book points out the value in life's simplest things. When life does not go as planned and we're hit with surprises, the solutions can be found in nature and in ourselves. Use this book when you've hit a troubling spot, or if you are curious to see from a backward (yet progressive) view.

"5.0 out of 5 stars Gentle Wisdom for the Heart, Mind, and Soul The author has an easy-to-understand way of writing even on some of these more difficult and abstract topics. She gently and kindly encourages us to explore our mental patterns that may or may not be working for us and those around us."

2023 NOTE FROM JANINE

Dear reader, I write for fellow souls who want and need information given outside of mainstream religious thought and outside of the 20+ billion dollar Adoption and Child Welfare Market. Despite adoption's widespread acceptance worldwide, many adult-adoptee grassroots groups are joining the effort to raise previously private concerns about the secret consequences of international adoption for all parties involved.

If you have ever wondered what adoption agencies are *not* telling you outside of the heartwarming stories, you will want to keep reading my adoption books intended for adults. In the next chapter of my writing career, I investigate hidden information that can help readers avoid unethical and even unconstitutional practices.

Did you know that only ten out of 50 states in the United States permit domestic-born adult adoptees unrestricted access to their original birth certificates? Adoption laws have altered the identities of an estimated five to seven million domestic-born adult adoptees and an estimated one million overseas adoptees worldwide since World War II, violating their God-given inherent, civil, and constitutional rights that all other humans enjoy.

The adoptee-rights movement in the US consists of determined domestic, late-discovery, and overseas intercountry adult adoptees. Due to only recently discovering how adoption violates innate human rights, their concerns have yet to scratch the surface.

Since the manufacture of adoption law was initially set up by religious entities founded on draconian ideas (claimed to be "of God" or "of Jesus" --but are not) and perpetuated by social services throughout its history, compounded by the immediate and fierce silencing and reprimanding of adopted people from speaking truth to power – even into our elder years, adopted people are now banning together to give voice to the crisis.

The mission and purpose of my collection of books for adults and the group that my sister and I formed in 2011 (Adoption Truth & Transparency Worldwide Information Network ATTWIN) will always be to educate the public in the effort to protect local and global children from being unnecessarily and permanently separated from their families—as we have been. Based on generations of experience, adoption law violates inherent God-given and natural human rights.

If you are a US citizen, we ask that you advocate for the US-based adoption lobby and governments to respect that all other nations have ratified the United Nations Convention on the Rights of the Child (UNCRC). Advocating for ratification is the most effective tool for the adoptee-rights movement. In contrast, adoption laws, such as the Hague Adoption Convention (HAC), ignore child rights and cements the commodification of children above the child's inherent God-given and natural human rights enshrined in the treaty to their own biological family, their community, and country of birth. To ensure child rights worldwide, please petition the US government to — at the very least — respect the rights of the people from other nations. Thank you for your consideration on this matter,

If you are and human-rights activist, advocate (ancestor or angel), or ally, we ask you to be the first to write an encouraging review for this effort on the book's "review" page. A show of support -- even a few words of encouragement -- helps us to fight against the now annual $20+ billion "Adoption and Child Welfare" worldwide industry. We live in a time now where most adoptees are ridiculed and persecuted for publicly sharing experiences. I hope the painful lifelong effort outshines the criticisms that can be easily dished out against those of us advocating for equal rights.

Curator,

Janine Vance
Adoption Books for Adults
AdoptionHistory.org

PS We have finally reached the age of truth & transparency! Isn't this great?

OTHER WORKS INCLUDE:

JANINEVANCE.COM

SCREENPLAYS: A fiction series on "For the Love of Children"

PERSONAL:
- *The Search for Mother Missing: A Peek Inside International Adoption* (Janine's 1st trip to Korea)
- *Twins Found in a Box: Adapting to Adoption 2003* (Janine's first book inspired by personal childhood experiences)
- *Adoption Stories: Excerpts from Adoption Books for Adults*

PHILOSOPHY:
- *Going Back to Zen*
- *The Power of Isolation*
- *Rise from the Dread*
- *Grief Relief* (A coloring book for adults)

ANTHOLOGIES:
Adoptionland: From Orphans to Activists
The "Unknown" Culture Club: Korean Adoptees, Then and Now

EMPOWERMENT:
- *Master Adoption: Claim Your Authentic Power*

RESEARCH:
- *Adoption: What You Should Know* (Textbook Edition: Adoption History)
- *Adoptopia: The Life & Times of Adoptive Father & Cult Leader, the Rev. Jim Jones*

DIRECTOR:
- *Against Child Trafficking's Adoption Trafficking Awareness Symposium*

KOREAN ADOPTEES WORLDWIDE

This collection serves as a tribute to transracially adopted people sent all over the world. It has been hailed to be the first book to give Korean adoptees the opportunity to speak freely since the pioneering of intercountry adoption after the Korean War. If you were adopted, you are not alone. These stories validate the experiences of all those who have been ridiculed or abused but have found the will to survive, thrive, and share their tale.

This book is a living testament to why previous "orphans" do not endorse the profitable Evangelical Orphan Movement (EOM). Those who work in the human rights field will see the value of this book. These courageous narratives could save you tens of thousands of dollars or prevent you from obtaining a stolen child.

"This is a powerful and important read for all. The adoptee voice is all too often silenced, and it can literally be life or death for some to be heard and seen." **AMAZON REVIEWER**

"Excellent for those that have experienced transracial adoption and for those of us that love and support them. It opens your eyes to their world and feelings." **AMAZON REVIEWER**

FOR YOUR ENCOURAGEMENT & YOUR EMPOWERMENT

Need to recover from adoption, but want an unusual philosophy outside of the Evangelical Orphan Movement (EOM) and more in tune with your inherent human rights and the natural law of identity? This short book is based on innate rights and presents philosophical ideas for those of us who got caught by the EOM and did NOT sign the contract to be obtained for overseas adoption.

"If you are adopted or have any connection to adoption, this is a must-read book. I was damaged by international adoption in the mid-1970s and this book provided validation and healing along with a deep look into the history of adoption practices and the harm that adopters and adoptioneers can cause, intentionally or not."

AMAZON REVIEWER

AGAINST CHILD TRAFFICKING
FIRST ADOPTION TRAFFICKING
AWARENESS SYMPOSIUM IN THE USA

"When I was asked to be the Master of Ceremonies for this conference [Adoption Trafficking Awareness Symposium] by its program director, Janine Vance, I had no idea what would actually evolve. As an international talk show host and producer, I interview hundreds of people a year from all walks of life, with all kinds of experiences on all levels. To hear the stories of individuals from around the world who have been subject to the traumas of being kidnapped, sold, and other sundry happenings, was incredible. Open discussion was encouraged and when all was shared, said, and done, the demeanor of hope filled the entire auditorium. It was an amazing and insightful gathering of people who realized they were not alone in their concerns and that there are answers/solutions for the international challenges that have existed for far too long. I hope that this conference will be repeated again."

~Donna Seebo, International radio host

WHAT ADULT ADOPTEES ARE SAYING

For adoption narratives from several points of view, including adoptees yesterday and around the world, grab *Adoptionland: From Orphans to Activists*.

"The Most important book of this century."

⭐⭐⭐⭐⭐ **AMAZON REVIEWER**

"Wow, this is a must-read for anyone that occupies this planet!"

⭐⭐⭐⭐⭐ **AMAZON REVIEWER**

"...I just finished re-reading it and I am completely blown away (again) at the breathtaking scope of voices. I am so thoroughly moved. If ONLY this book had been available to me to read when I was a much younger adoptee in the depths of pain and lost in the adoption fog and fear. This book would've educated me on adoptionland, that what I was feeling was shared with other adoptees. Reading this in my 20s - after I opened my adoption with a judge, I would have felt less isolated, less alone...."

⭐⭐⭐⭐⭐ **AMAZON REVIEWER**

"A must-read for social workers, therapists, and anyone interested in adoption!"

⭐⭐⭐⭐⭐ **AMAZON REVIEWER**

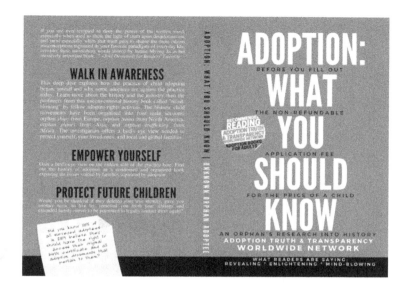

INFORMATION IS YOUR SECRET SUPERPOWER:

You need to know how adoption began and spread and why more and more adoptees are against the practice today. Learn more about the history and the industry than the professionals in the field from *Adoption: What You Should Know*. This unconventional history book has been called mind-blowing by fellow adoptee-rights activists. The main movements of children are organized into four sections and referred to as orphan ships (Europe), orphan trains (America), orphan planes (Asia), and orphan trafficking (Africa). *Fellow adoptee rights activists have called the book "Revealing," "Enlightening," and "Mindblowing." Also available on audiobook.

TEXTBOOK VERSION WITH BONUS MATERIAL

To provide comfort and care for trauma survivors, *Adoption: What You Should Know* is also available in this original Hardcover Textbook Edition titled *Adoption History: An Adoptee's Research Into Child Trafficking*. This version was awarded five stars and won silver at the Readers' Favorite International Book Award Ceremony in the Non-Fiction Gov/Politics Category. It also includes "Only in Adoption" survey results from domestic, late-discovery, transracial, and overseas adoptees.

WHAT YOU DON'T KNOW COULD HURT YOU

"I took advantage of the holidays to read *Adoption: What You Should Know*. It was an eye-opening experience. Actually, it continues to be an eye-opening experience because I find myself going back to the details of the historical sections time and again.

I very much like that the book places so much emphasis on historical developments, which are also aptly presented as global phenomena. They bring home even more strongly that adoption transports own, by now, a very long, under-researched, and nefarious history.

On the latter subject the author is clear in her objectives: creating awareness, inspiring action, guiding reform that must include the voices of the adoptees themselves. Warmly recommended! A marker of the turning tide in adoption literature, now that adult adoptees are finding their own voices and creating their own forums. As a movement, that, too, is to be commended."

Gonda Van Steen, author of
Adoption, Memory, and Cold War Greece

★ ★ ★ ★ ★ **AMAZON REVIEWER**

ABOUT THE VANCE TWINS TODAY

Twin sisters, now known as Jenette and Janine Vance, were claimed to have been abandoned on a South Korean street in 1972. They believed this assertion written in their adoption file for over thirty years. The adoption agency alleged they were discovered, and the twins were taken to be processed for overseas adoption and raised in a typical American family fraught with unusual challenges, ups, downs, and additional burdens.

The Vance twins recently learned at age fifty that their adoptions had been "illegal and a serious human rights violation," according to a recent research report by South Korea's Truth and Reconciliation Commission initiated by Korean adoptees worldwide. The findings confirmed their suspicions that the adoption agency sourced children en masse and profited greatly.

After the twins' adoptive mother died from cancer in 1997, Janine became curious about their adoption story. At age twenty-five, she started researching and discovered that many international adoptions were often marred by corruption, fraud, and injustice. Janine's curiosity turned insatiable; Vance became a full-time researcher and writer determined to unravel the truth about how children from around the world had been obtained for adoption. She wrote extensively about its history, the aftermath and concerns of the people most impacted, including families separated by adoption. Several of Janine's books have won international acclaim from book clubs and contests.

Jenette took a different career path. She worked in the healthcare field for more than twenty-five years. Throughout those years, she encouraged Janine's research and would often help her market her articles and books. The twins established a forum in 2011 called Adoption Truth and Transparency Worldwide Information Network (ATTWIN). They invited domestic, late-discovery, transracial, and overseas adoptees to participate, families separated-by-adoption, and parents-of-loss to discuss adoption-related concerns.

The twins use ATTWIN to privately collaborate with adult adoptee-led groups and to stay informed. Each member raises awareness in their unique way based on personal experience impacted by adoption. The sisters discuss their observations and use their shared knowledge and skills to protect local and global families from adoption trafficking.

Jenette and Janine's story is not just about adoption but about the power of siblings, resilience, and the importance of using one's belief to fight for what is right. They are a testament to the fact that even in the most difficult circumstances, one can pioneer a path and make a meaningful impact on the world.

Why has the adoption market remained in full force worldwide? Information has been suppressed since the manufacture of adoption law spearheaded, maintained, and monitored by adoption pioneers, profiteers, and their loyal customer base. Janine's Adoption Books for Adults offer vital and often secretive information that can be difficult to find.

VANCE accepts written interviews at
contact@janinevance.com or info@adoptionhistory.org
contact Janine's twin at jenette@vancetwins.com

THE COVER IMAGE
BY DARIUSXSTUDIO.COM

Darius X is an Artist, Printmaker, Korean Adoptee, Transguy, Musician, Lover, Fighter, Pansy, Extroverted Introvert, Taurus, and part-time Pet Portraitist. He has been exploring his passion for printmaking for over 20 years. Working primarily with lino prints, Darius creates large-scale self-portraits, landscapes, and other musings on his life as a Transgender Korean Adoptee. Since 2017 he has been working with mixed-media installations. At that time, he collaborated with Flynn Bickley in an interactive diorama installation titled *Procedures for Entering Enclosed Spaces*. In 2018, he collaborated with Clyde Petersen on a cardboard guitar extravaganza show titled *Shredders*.

He is a teaching artist, having taught printmaking, interactive mixed-media design for emerging LGBTQ+ artists, and continues to work at his primary job at Apple as a technology trainer.

He has exhibited throughout the Pacific Northwest, Nelson, BC, Seoul, S. Korea, Oakland, CA, and St. Paul, MN, and has collaborated with several Seattle based Queer, Trans, and people of color communities, including The Wing Luke Asian American Museum, IDEA Odyssey Art Gallery, QPOC Liberation Project and The Bamboo Clan.

His artwork can be found on the cover of three books by adoptee and child trafficking activist Janine Myung Ja; *Adoptionland: From Orphans to Activists*, *The Search for Mother Missing*, and *Adoption History 101: an Orphan's Research*. In 2016 he opened a small storefront studio in the Beacon Hill neighborhood in Seattle, WA, where he creates art, hosts community events, and sells his work.

SUGGESTED RESOURCES

POLITICS & HISTORY:
WWW.ADOPTIONHISTORY.ORG

ADOPTION BOOKS FOR ADULTS:
HTTPS://ADOPTIONBOOKS.ORG

BRIDGING THE CULTURAL GAP:
WWW.KOREANADOPTEESWORLDWIDE.NET

FOR ADOPTEES ONLY:
WWW.ADOPTIONTRUTH.ORG

GLOBAL ADOPTION NEWS:
WWW.ADOPTIONLAND.ORG

MAKING FUN OF ADOPTION:
WWW.ADOPTOPIA.ORG

VANCE FAMILY'S FAVORITE CHARITY:
WWW.AGAINSTCHILDTRAFFICKING.ORG
USA.AGAINSTCHILDTRAFFICKING.ORG

JANINE'S PERSONAL & PHILOSOPHY:
WWW.JANINEVANCE.COM

FUN WITH VANCE TWINS:
WWW.VANCETWINS.COM

Made in the USA
Monee, IL
10 January 2024